made in morocco

PENGUIN BOOKS

made in morocco

A JOURNEY OF EXOTIC TASTES & PLACES

Ackley Public Library
401 State Street
Ackley, Iowa 50601

HARISSA

30 DH

JULIE LE CLERC

AN UNFORGETTABLE FIRST IMPRESSION: MOSQUE HASSAN II, MESMERISINGLY SPOTLIT UNDER A SHAFT OF SUNLIGHT THAT HAD ESCAPED FROM AN OTHERWISE GREY, EARLY MORNING SKY.

It floated two kilometres away at the end of the white-washed old medina, with nothing but endless sea and sky beyond. Great flocks of birds whirled around the minarets, light danced off the finials. I stood transfixed, wondering if this spectacular was being staged for me alone.

In the time that it took to grab a map, which confirmed the true identity of this vision, the shaft of light had enlarged to illuminate the whole of the medina. A lone palm tree stood tall, verdant and sentinel, its large mop of deep green fronds in contrast to the dense mass of satellite dishes, fixed in groups on every roof-top patio. These incongruous icons of the contemporary world seemed to be shouldered reluctantly by the mud-brick buildings of a past era that knelt below them.

The view before me was not from any guide book that I had read. This Casablanca medina was bursting with post-dawn vitality; countless hues of white seeping from the crush of buildings set forth a shimmering aura of expectation. It oozed an age much older than the pubescent French-ordained city that corralled it.

I opened the windows to be immediately wrapped in the din of everyday life. Remarkably, I had slept through the muezzin's calls to prayer, but the cries of children, shopkeepers and donkeys, ancient vans, taxis and mopeds drifted through my window like a salve of confirmation that this day would be like any other in Casablanca. Improvised lines of washing were being hung out to dry from windows and across patios. Trays of tea were being whisked by boys to shops for their waiting keepers and customers alike. Produce was barrowed, carried and toted on heads to all corners of the market. For at least an hour, this was the most fascinating thing that I had ever witnessed.

But I soon learned that Morocco was full of contrasts: the humble donkey with a heroic load, tottering along a truck-infested highway; men wearing traditional djellabahs over the latest European-designed suits; satellite dishes staked atop 1000-year-old buildings; invariably, the very old alongside the very new.

Perhaps this explains why those who visit Morocco recount their travels with hushed, almost breathless excitement. This aura surrounding Morocco was something that I had long mulled over in the quiet of my 'where to next' travel dreams. I didn't have to mull for long. A chance meeting in my publisher's office with food writer Julie Le Clerc, as she was putting the final touches to her seventh cookbook, led me to ask her what was the latest travel destination for gastro-nomads? 'Morocco', was the swift reply.

And the seeds of an amazing journey were sewn. Six months later, a little travelling party left New Zealand, determined to photograph and taste their way around this beguiling country: Julie Le Clerc, my wife Anna, and father-in-law Graeme, all very seasoned travellers, all with very different expectations. For me it was to let Morocco build upon my memorable first impression, Julie wanted to see and taste the food in its natural location. Anna, with her 'Berber woman' negotiating ability, stepped into the role of prop collector with ease, and Graeme was simply content to be a bon vivant in a strange and exotic land. Julie would immerse herself in researching the local food and I would photograph everything worthy of having a camera pointed at it. We would all live together in everything from traditional riads, to kasbahs and ornate boutique hotels; cook, eat, shop and explore. And although you can always rely on the unexpected when travelling in spite of meticulous planning, Morocco fulfilled our separate dreams. JB

العشواء المراكشي

150,00 درهم

رأس الغنم كبير 60.00 درهم

رأس الغنم صغير 50 درهم

طنجية لكيلو 120 درهم

طنجية عند كيلو 60 درهم

طاجين صغير 20.00 درهم

براد الشاي من 3 إلى 10 درهم

مرحبا بكم عندنا

WHISPERING OF THE PAST WITH HAUNTING PERFUMES AND BEGUILING FLAVOURS; INVITING TOUCH THROUGH TEXTURAL RICHNESS AND DECORATION – MOROCCAN FOOD WEAVES A SPELL THAT COMPLETELY ENGAGES ALL THE SENSES.

After years of cooking and eating many delicious renditions of Moroccan food, I found myself spellbound by the other-worldly allure of this cuisine. I realised that I desperately wanted to hear the cacophony and see the vibrancy of Morocco's culinary landscape for myself. As a professional cook and food writer, I needed to experience the preparation of time-honoured recipes under the guidance of traditional cooks. I hungered to smell and touch the raw ingredients and to eat genuine dishes in the place of their inception. I wanted to be immersed in this land steeped in history, to research and to investigate, and above all, to taste. These notions continued to feed the yearning I had long felt to discover the real food of Morocco, first-hand.

And then, just like magic, I met talented photographer and intrepid adventurer John Bougen. Our fortuitous encounter revealed that we shared a great passion for exotic travel and, importantly, culinary experiences and photography. The magnetic pull of curiosity fixed the decision that we would take our time and explore Morocco at length. Four of us set off on a cook's tour of this ancient land to discover, eat and cook authentic dishes, meet the locals and to capture the food, ingredients and vibrant atmosphere photographically.

Travelling around Morocco proved to be a justly fascinating and constantly stimulating voyage of discovery. As anticipated, many of the greatest pleasures we enjoyed came from experiencing real Moroccan cooking, which is truly distinctive and beguiling. One of the aspects of Moroccan food that makes it so special is the sensual harmony that these dishes hold. Consider a hauntingly perfumed tagine as an example of harmonious composition. To eat a tagine by touch, dipping the fingers of one hand into this warm, perfectly balanced dish, which is savoury yet sweet on the palate, and enigmatically

spiced and intricately aromatic to the nose, is to partake of a meal that involves all the senses.

Moroccan food is truly food of the heart; and it is food of the land, sea and sky. In many ways we did not discover anything completely new – this is intensely traditional food after all; it is very much as you would expect it to be. However, for me, there is nothing more extraordinary than eating authentic food in the country of its origin. And to experience the effort involved in creating some of Morocco's most remarkable signature dishes, such as couscous or b'stilla, is to witness Morocco's past reflected in its rich culinary traditions.

Moroccan recipes possess a strong taste of history. Based on the old foods and traditions of the indigenous Berber inhabitants, Moroccan cuisine also resonates with unique tastes brought by waves of invaders. Muslim Arabs introduced spectacular spices gathered from far Asian trade routes and today a distinctly Persian inheritance can be seen in the way Moroccan recipes incorporate elaborate multiple spice blends.

The Arabs also brought with them a love of opulence and sensuality. They introduced perfumed, decorative, jewelled food and exotic practices, such as the ideas of fusing sweet with sour, and meat with fruit. Moroccans happily embraced these tastes and adornments. Later, when the Arab Moors were driven from Spain, they returned to Morocco with new culinary habits embellished with Spanish traits. The production of olive oil is one of the important influences gathered from Spain. And more recently, the French left legacies of fancy pastries, desserts and winemaking.

In Morocco, food is considered to be a powerful and symbolic substance; and not just in the culinary sense. Moroccans hold food in the highest regard, maintaining the belief that sharing food honours visitors, friends and family. Generosity is demonstrated through serving certain ingredients, such as meat, dates, or mint tea made with lots of sugar (sugar was once very expensive).

Furthermore, food is invested with significant religious meaning. Certain dishes are eaten in relation to the religious calendar; couscous for instance, is served on Fridays, as Friday is a holy day. The Prophet Mohammed proclaimed food to be sacred so it must be shown absolute respect. This is why bread, the most basic staff of life, is particularly honoured by Moroccans. People will rescue from harm's way a discarded crust of bread lying in the street, kiss it and thank Allah for the gift of bread.

The souk forms the heart of Moroccan life and offers baskets full of culinary inspiration. Of all the mesmerising ingredients in the souk, the kaleidoscope of heady spices are quite possibly the most magical. Some combination spice blends, such as the famous and extremely complex ras el hanout, reach almost mystical proportions. The way that spices are used by Moroccan cooks certainly transcends the ordinary. When added with an intuitive hand, these aromatics delicately infuse dishes with a haunting complexity and eloquence that is hard to surpass.

For me, it is this clever use of basic and familiar ingredients that makes Moroccan cooking so striking. While many everyday ingredients are completely ordinary, some are truly exceptional. Consider couscous, the hand-rolled, elusively scented grains of golden semolina that are steamed until delectably soft and fluffy. Then there's saffron, the dried stigmas of crocus flowers plucked before dawn; lemons preserved in salt; and divinely perfumed flower waters, being the distilled culinary essence of pure roses or orange blossoms. These bewitching components are uniquely utilised in Moroccan recipes to turn very simple food into something outstanding.

As it is for many authentic cuisines of the world, the real food of Morocco occurs in the home. Its creation takes place behind closed doors, in the kitchens of the people. So, it was in home kitchens that we happily found ourselves immersed in the preparation of authentic dishes. Traditionally, written recipes are not common. Moroccan recipes are inherited experiences that are passed down like an incantation or intimate sign language through the hands and minds of generations of cooks in the same family. I am therefore deeply grateful to have had the opportunity to learn from Moroccan home cooks. I sincerely thank these wonderful individuals for sharing with me their knowledge, skill, time and generosity of spirit, and, of course, for sharing their glorious recipes.

Many of the recipes in this book were composed from experiencing Moroccan food first-hand, and from my taste memories. Some recipes are my own creations – modern renditions influenced by the magical ingredients of Morocco. Moroccan cooks kindly demonstrated other recipes – to be understood, certain nuances had to be observed, felt and tasted before the recipe could be translated onto paper. I found that I was constantly scribbling notes, detailing some unique alteration, eccentricity, or some special information gained from a local cook or dining experience.

I was fascinated to observe that within the bounds of custom, Moroccan cuisine has been delightfully personalised. Recipes vary from person to person; each cook will add innovations to slightly alter a dish and infuse it with their own sensual style. Cooks will maintain, of course, that their version is the most authentic and delicious. In a similar fashion I have made my own adaptations to some recipes, while still honouring traditions and retaining integrity of flavour.

Wherever possible I have adjusted recipes to make them more approachable to modern cooks, who are sometimes challenged by time constraints. It is my hope that these recipes will offer a chance to gain knowledge of the true methods and cuisine of Morocco, while the less complicated methods will make preparation easier for the non-Moroccan home cook.

Today, Moroccan cuisine is extremely popular outside of Morocco where there is a wide enthusiasm for replicating these spectacular flavours. Delicatessens and even supermarkets stock couscous and other integral Moroccan ingredients. Condiments, such as harissa and preserved lemons, can be found in specialty food stores or easily recreated at home. The ready availability of authentic raw ingredients brings all the flavours and smells of the souk to the global kitchen. The following recipes will in turn bring the sensually engaging food of Morocco to your own table.

I hope that you will be enticed to cook these magical dishes, relish the perfumed tastes, and take your own enchanted voyage via your taste-buds. JLEC

casablanca

OF ALL THE CITIES IN MOROCCO, Casablanca is the best known, thanks almost entirely to being immortalised as an exotic colonial outpost in the Hollywood movie of the same name. Today, Casablanca is no longer a sleepy outpost, but bustles between the practices of ancient times and the rapid adoption of the latest technological advances.

Present-day Casablanca owes much to the French. Prior to their establishing Morocco as a French protectorate, the city had been under the control of a succession of foreign occupiers, ever since the Berber settlement of Anfa (now the most élite suburb of Casablanca) was sacked by the Arabs in AD 683.

The port has long been Casablanca's key asset, with evidence of Phoenicians visiting in the seventh century BC and the Romans around 15 BC. During the fifteenth century, Casablanca enjoyed a sustained period of notoriety on account of its pirate ships, which plundered homeward-bound Spanish and Portuguese galleons. The Portuguese, however, finally took exception when pirate ships started hunting off the Port of Lisbon. Their succinct reprisal, the sacking of Anfa in 1468, ended the marauding.

In 1770, the re-establishment of Anfa began in earnest on the decree of Sultan Sidi Mohammed Ben Abdallah. To commemorate its rebuilding and subsequent conversion to Islam, the Sultan renamed Anfa, Dar el Beida (White House or Casa Blanca in Spanish). The port once again became a principal point of export for corn, grain, sugar, wool and tea. The population grew rapidly with an influx of European settlers, although it was still only a mere eight thousand by the mid-nineteenth century.

The Casablanca of 1912 was still contained within the walls of what is now known as the old medina. France's decision to establish Casablanca as the economic hub of Morocco heralded a new direction for a town that had plodded along for over a thousand years.

The port was expanded, and town planners delighted in designing a city on what was effectively bare land. Architects and developers constructed with gusto. However, this all paled into insignificance with the great building boom of the 1930s. This time the city was gripped by a development fever, the like of which will never be seen again. Architects from France and its territories of Algeria and Tunisia designed richly decorated buildings, incorporating Art Nouveau and Art Deco details, embellished with motifs from Renaissance, Neoclassical and Moorish traditions. Much of this work remains today. Another French decision was to have a major effect on the growth of Casablanca. In order to preserve Morocco's existing cities, all new constsruction was to be undertaken outside the city walls. While the tourist of today may be overjoyed to see cities such as Fez and Marrakech as they were centuries ago, it wasn't considered a good environment for the inhabitants left within the walls — they were fast becoming living museum exhibits. Gradually these inhabitants moved to the new towns or to the coastal cities of Casablanca and Rabat, along with the poor country dwellers lured by the prospect of employment, thus accelerating Casablanca's current population to over four million. The end result of this unplanned influx of inhabitants is the town planning and social problems for which the city has now become infamous.

However, there is much that appeals. A tour of the central city reveals a plethora of splendidly preserved Art Deco and Art Nouveau-style buildings. Numerous new shopping areas have evolved and contrary to popular belief there are a multitude of restaurants that offer a choice in both standard and price.

A visit to Mosque Hassan II is essential. Named after Hassan II, the father of the current King Mohammed VI, the mosque commemorates his position as a spiritual leader of the Muslims of Morocco and fulfilled his desire for the city to be given a heart. Built entirely by donations from the people of Morocco, at times the level of contributions were so high they temporarily drained Morocco's money supply.

This mosque, second in size only to its counterpart in Mecca, has the tallest minaret in the world at 200 metres. Positioned majestically on the coast, and covering nine acres of land in total, it is built two-thirds over water in adherence to the Islamic belief that 'the throne of God is over land and water'. On any day but Friday, Muslims and unbelievers alike are welcome to pass through one of the twelve electronically raised doors and gaze in awe over the prayer room. Here, 25,000 worshippers (plus 80,000 on the forecourt) can be accommodated. Above the three-acre central prayer room, an electronically operated retracting roof can be opened to offer a view of the heavens. The structure's hues change with majestic grace as the day progresses to night, at which time, from up to thirty kilometres away, its location can be fixed by the twin laser beams shining in the direction of Mecca; hence it is also known as the Lighthouse of Islam. JB

THE LUMINOUS LIGHT OF SUNRISE casts a golden glow over the pale city of Casablanca as the wail of the muezzin calls the faithful to prayer. We awaken with the knowledge that we are somewhere distinctly different. We have arrived in Morocco, at last.

Our first morning in this fascinating land is full of culinary revelations, as we breakfast on dishes I've never encountered before. Our buffet is set with an array of traditional breakfast breads and a large suspended sheet of honeycomb that releases a flow of perfumed honey onto a pewter tray.

There are piles of semolina pancakes, possessing a lacy, honeycomb texture, reminiscent of crumpets. These yeasted delights, called beghrir, are cooked in a skillet, on one side only, then lavishly drenched in butter and honey. One taste and beghrir immediately became my favourite Moroccan breakfast dish. Other traditional breakfast breads include harsha – cake-like semolina flatbreads that resemble English muffins; mlaoui and msammen are equally alluring treats. These flat packages of thinly rolled dough are folded and interleaved with oil or butter, then fried to create flaky pastry-textured parcels that are also served with lashings of honey.

Some mornings we venture out to breakfast in a local café. Here we start the day with glasses of scented thé à la menthe (mint tea) or excellent espresso coffee. Juice squeezed from famous Royal Moroccan oranges, or blood orange juice that is deep crimson in colour and a little more tart in flavour, is another enticement. We watch what the Moroccan clientele order and follow their lead. Individual earthenware tagines are delivered to our tables, the conical lids are whisked away and we are presented with dishes of poached eggs and salted meat.

This is khlie, a specialty, we are told, of Casablanca and Fez. In this dish, meat that has been preserved in salt is first cooked in fat, then eggs are fried around the morsels of meat (see page 23). This is simple rustic food and a very delicious combination, where the meat imparts a delicious saltiness to the eggs. Any runny-egg juices are sopped up with scraps of warm flatbread that we soon discover is ubiquitous to meals in Morocco. Filled with this hearty breakfast, we are now ready to explore the city's medina and souks.

The past and the present exist side by side in Casablanca's medina. In many ways it is like stepping back in time – the daily rituals are constant; the cobbled lanes are ancient and worn –

and yet every modern item of clothing and designer accessory are available in the souk.

As we explore the alleyways of the medina we are invariably welcomed with the French greeting 'Bienvenue'. Stall-holders also say 'Welcome to Morocco' and touch their right hand to their heart to demonstrate their heartfelt gesture of sincerity. A child selling bread and pastries from a humble wooden handcart welcomes us simply with a smile.

Long shadows merge with glittering sunlight as it plays on the uncovered central square where the shoeshine men ply their trade. There are various street food stalls in the square and the odd mobile vendor can be found along the pathways of the souk. We pass a glass-encased mobile cart containing dishes of couscous and almond milk, which are dispensed into bowls taken from an upside-down stack perched on top of the cart.

My favourite culinary vision is the marketplace cook selling escargots. He has a colourful and elaborately painted cart, topped with a vat of snails simmering in a spice-flavoured broth. An orange stuck with bent safety-pins sits beside the vat – eaters use the pins to extract the snails from their shells. While I am not game enough to try his specialty dish, I enjoy watching his steady trade of happy customers warming their hands on small china bowls holding their portion of steaming snail-filled broth.

Down a lane, deep in the shade, hidden and mysterious, lies a cluster of small cafés. These medina eateries appear almost medieval and consist of a few chairs placed around a worn table, a miniature kitchen space with tiled walls and one gas ring or charcoal brazier for cooking. They sell staple dishes of harira, brochettes and simple tagines to hungry lunchtime diners. We also observe tagines being whisked from these kitchens and through the lanes of the souk to waiting stall-holders.

We are invited to sip mint tea with a vendor of tiny, opulently coloured Moroccan tea glasses and beaten silver teapots. This experience will be the first of many. Over the weeks we will be offered mint tea time and again, even during moments of frenetic bartering.

I wander to the spice souk and gather a stash of essentials. I choose a mixed combination of spices to make meat dishes aromatic and savoury: Moroccan saffron to colour and scent couscous; flower waters to perfume sweets; and semolina so that I can replicate beghrir, my favourite Moroccan breakfast. JLEC

sweet couscous with dates and pistachio nuts

IN MOROCCO, THIS DISH IS MOST LIKELY TO BE SERVED AT SPECIAL CELEBRATIONS. HOWEVER, I FIND THAT AS AN ALTERNATIVE FORM OF CEREAL IT MAKES PERFECT BREAKFAST FOOD.

1 cup instant couscous

finely stripped zest of 1 orange

1 cup orange juice

3 tablespoons honey

1/2 teaspoon ground cinnamon

1 teaspoon orange flower water

1 tablespoon olive oil

1 cup pitted fresh dates

1/4 cup chopped pistachio nuts

yoghurt and extra honey to serve

1 Place couscous in a bowl. Place orange zest and juice in a saucepan and bring to the boil. Add honey to dissolve in hot orange juice. Add cinnamon, orange flower water and olive oil.

2 Pour this hot liquid over the couscous, stir to combine and cover tightly with plastic wrap. Set aside to steam for 10 minutes.

3 Fluff up steamed couscous with a fork; stir through dates and pistachio nuts. Serve topped with yoghurt and drizzled with honey.

SERVES 4

honeycomb pancakes

THESE YEASTED SEMOLINA PANCAKES (CALLED BEGHRIR IN MOROCCAN) ARE DELICIOUSLY INTRIGUING. THEY ARE COOKED ON ONE SIDE ONLY AND TURN OUT BUBBLY AND LACY IN APPEARANCE, A LITTLE LIKE CRUMPETS. THEY ARE THE PERFECT VEHICLES FOR LASHINGS OF HONEY. WE ATE THIS BREAKFAST TREAT ALL OVER MOROCCO AND, ONCE TRIED, THEY INSTANTLY BECAME A FAVOURITE. WE GIVE MANY THANKS TO THE STAFF AT THE PALAIS SALAM HOTEL IN TAROUDANNT FOR FEEDING US SO WELL AND GIFTING US WITH THIS PRIZED RECIPE.

1/4 cup warm water

1 tablespoon active dried yeast

2 teaspoons sugar

1 cup fine semolina

1 cup plain flour

1/2 teaspoon salt

1 teaspoon vanilla extract

1 egg, lightly beaten

13/4 cups tepid water

vegetable oil, such as sunflower oil, for frying

butter to serve

comb honey to serve

1   Place warm water in a small bowl and sprinkle with yeast and then sugar. Set aside in a warm place to activate for 5–10 minutes (when activated the mixture will be frothy).

2   Place the semolina, flour and salt in a large bowl and make a well in the centre. Pour in the frothy yeast mixture, vanilla, beaten egg and tepid water and mix to form a smooth and creamy batter. Cover and set batter aside for 1 hour.

3   When ready to cook pancakes, preheat a non-stick frying pan or skillet over a medium heat. Brush the pan with a thin coating of oil. Stir mixture until smooth, then ladle a spoonful of batter into the pan and cook without turning until the surface has become full of holes and dry, and the base is golden brown.

4   Remove pancake and continue making pancakes with the remaining mixture, adding a little more oil to the pan for each.

5   Serve hot slathered with butter and comb honey.

MAKES 20

fried pastry squares

ALL OVER MOROCCO, DELICIOUS SWEET PASTRY-LIKE CREATIONS CALLED MLAOUI OR MSAMMEN ARE MADE FOR BREAKFAST OR SOLD AS STREET FOOD THAT CAN BE ENJOYED AT ANY TIME OF THE DAY. MLAOUI ARE A LITTLE COMPLICATED TO REPLICATE, BEING INTRICATELY THIN PASTRY THAT IS LAYERED AND PAN-FRIED UNTIL CRISP. HOWEVER, ONCE YOU GET THE KNACK AND A TASTE FOR THEM SERVED HOT WITH LASHINGS OF HONEY, THERE'LL BE NO STOPPING YOU.

1 cup plain flour

1 cup fine semolina

1/4 teaspoon sea salt

1 cup warm water

extra sunflower oil

50g butter

2 tablespoons sunflower oil

honey to serve

1 Sift flour, semolina and salt into a large bowl and make a well in the centre. Add just enough of the measured water to make a stiff dough. Knuckle in remaining water and knead and stretch the dough with your hands in the bowl until it is smooth and elastic.

2 Divide the dough into 8 golf ball-sized portions. Rub the balls with a little sunflower oil and set aside to rest for 15 minutes. Melt the butter and combine with 2 tablespoons sunflower oil.

3 On a work surface, flatten each ball with your hand into a very thin disc about 20cm in diameter. Lightly brush the surface with a little melted butter and oil mix. Fold one-third into the middle, then the next third over this, like a business letter. Rotate and fold in three the other way to obtain a pastry square. Repeat with remaining balls of dough. Set aside to rest for another 15 minutes.

4 Flatten parcels with your hand into 15cm squares and brush with a little more butter and oil mix. Heat a non-stick frying pan. Cook pastry squares over a moderate heat for 2–3 minutes on each side or until mottled golden brown.

5 Serve hot drizzled with a highly flavoured honey.

MAKES 8

berber omelette

THIS SPICY OMELETTE IS A GREAT DISH TO ENJOY IN A COMMUNAL FASHION. I THOROUGHLY RECOMMEND DRIZZLING THE SURFACE WITH OLIVE OIL AND USING WARM FLATBREAD TO MOP UP THE JUICES.

4 tablespoons olive oil

1 onion, finely chopped

1 teaspoon each ground turmeric, coriander and paprika

400g can tomatoes, chopped

6 eggs, lightly beaten

sea salt and freshly ground black pepper

extra virgin olive oil to serve

1 Heat an ovenproof frying pan or tagine, add olive oil and onion and cook over a medium heat for 10 minutes until softened. Add spices and fry for 1 minute to release their flavours.

2 Add chopped tomatoes and simmer for 10 minutes, stirring occasionally until liquid is reduced and the mixture thickened.

3 Remove from the heat, stir in beaten eggs and season with salt and pepper. Cover and transfer to the oven. Bake for 20–30 minutes or until puffed and set.

4 Argan oil was poured over the surface of this dish just before we ate it, but a strong-flavoured, quality extra virgin olive oil would make a fair substitute.

SERVES 4

egg and salted beef tagine

THIS TASTY BREAKFAST DISH, CALLED KHLIE, IS COMMONLY AVAILABLE FROM CAFÉS, ESPECIALLY IN FEZ AND CASABLANCA WHERE THE TRADITION OF BREAKFASTING OUT IS PREVALENT. KHLIE IS MADE WITH A SPECIALLY PREPARED BEEF, WHICH HAS BEEN PRESERVED (SALTED AND DRIED), THEN COOKED IN FAT AND WATER. AS THIS PREPARATION IS NOT ACCESSIBLE OUTSIDE OF MOROCCO, I'VE SUBSTITUTED CORNED BEEF AND OBTAINED EQUALLY DELICIOUS RESULTS. PANCETTA OR SLAB BACON ARE OTHER GOOD OPTIONS.

3 tablespoons olive oil

100g corned beef, roughly chopped

2 eggs

flatbread to serve

1 Heat the base of a tagine or a small frying pan, add oil and corned beef and gently fry for 1 minute.

2 Break eggs into the pan, cover and cook for 3–4 minutes until eggs are bubbling hot and cooked so that the yolks are still soft. Serve with bread to sop up the juices.

SERVES 1

coffee

Moroccans often make the comment that time is something they have in abundance. 'Time doesn't count in Morocco' or 'We have nothing but time' are regularly voiced philosophies. This notion is so refreshing to those who come from a culture where daily pressures combine to create a feeling that there is never enough time in a day to achieve what must be done. Moroccans have the luxury of time — and what's more, they take this time to enjoy the pleasures of life.

Coffee is one of these pleasures. While less popular than the national drink of mint tea, taking coffee is an extremely enjoyable pastime in Morocco. Even at the most humble of roadside cafés, espresso is expertly prepared. More often than not, coffee is served the French way — café noir (espresso) or café au lait (with milk). To blend with the locals, order kahwa nuss u nuss, meaning half-half, a perfect blend of espresso coffee and fluffy hot milk — delicious! JLEC

dried fig compote

DRIED APRICOTS, PRUNES, DATES, RAISINS OR A COMBINATION OF FRUITS CAN BE SUBSTITUTED FOR THE FIGS IN THIS RECIPE IF DESIRED.

2 cups dried figs
1 cinnamon stick
juice and pared rind of 1 lemon
juice of 1 orange
1 teaspoon rose water
1/2 cup sugar
cold water to cover

1   Combine all the ingredients in a bowl and pour over just enough water to cover the figs. Cover bowl and leave to stand overnight for the figs to soften.

2   Next day, transfer mixture to a large saucepan and bring to the boil. Turn down the heat and simmer for 10 minutes or until the liquid becomes syrupy.

3   Remove to a bowl to cool. Refrigerate until ready to serve.

SERVES 6

hand of fatima

Fatima, the daughter of the Muslim prophet, Mohammed, farewelled her two sons as they left to join their father in a holy war. She had just applied henna to her hands, so when she hugged them both goodbye the henna left imprints of her hands on their white robes. The war had not been going well until Fatima's sons, dressed in their pure white attire, entered the fray. On their first day in battle neither of Fatima's sons nor their comrades were killed or injured. This good fortune was attributed to the hand-prints seen clearly on the robes of both sons. To this day, the Hand of Fatima is deemed to be a harbinger of good luck and protection. JB

fez

LOOKING DOWN ON FEZ in the early morning light gives a sense of the impossibility of ever finding one's way around. Fez el Bali, the old city, is a seamless crush of taupe-hued buildings, interspersed with jade green-tiled roofs. The towers of the medina's 120 mosques stand proud and beckoning. Through the camera's lens, the whitewash that meets the naked eye transpires to be satellite dishes that crowd every rooftop, the only hint that the twenty-first century has arrived. Otherwise, the vista has remained unchanged since the city's foundation in the early ninth century.

Entering the historic city of Fez el Bali through one of the fourteen gates piercing the ramparts is a cataclysmic jolt to the senses – one is transported back centuries. Nothing has changed in terms of how daily life is conducted by the 200,000 inhabitants of this walled and cobblestoned city, other than the introduction of electricity and the occasional moped.

According to Rachid, our guide, the only way to get even the merest understanding of the layout and evolution of Fez is to drive up to Borj Sud (South Fort). Standing on the hill pondering the scene below, Rachid gently explains that the river Fez had been mostly built over. 'It still flows below,' he says, pointing out the main points of this tripartite city. To the right (east) of the river is the Andalous quarter (Fez el Andalous) named after the thousands of highly skilled, artisan, Andalucian Arab refugee families, who were given sanctuary here by Idriss II, son of the founder of Fez, in AD 808 after their expulsion from southern Spain. To the west of the river is the town built by Idriss II, populated by the arrival in AD 825 of a smaller number of Tunisian Muslim refugees.

It was Yousef ben Tachfine, the leader of Morocco, who in the eleventh century built the first wall that encompassed the towns on each side of the river. In addition, he decreed that mosques, public buildings, baths, markets and fountains should be built in the city along with accommodation for the ever-burgeoning numbers of traders and merchants. He also ordered the reticulation of water to every house.

When the Almohads took the city in 1150 they destroyed much of it. A mere generation later, seeing the error of their ways, they set about rebuilding what they had destroyed, including the immense city walls which stand defending Fez to this day.

By the thirteenth century Fez had a population of 125,000, with residents having at their disposal no less than 785 mosques, 9000 shops, 372 flour mills, 135 bread ovens as well a hundred fountains and as many public baths. The Merinids came in their thousands after conquering Spain, and a new town, Fez Jdid, was constructed to the west and above the old town.

The Merinids ruled in a largely philanthropic fashion through to 1465. After a series of ineffective rulers, the Saadians arrived in 1541 and, although they shifted the capital once again to the south, continued embellishing Fez thanks to their gold wealth acquired from lands south of Morocco. But by the mid-seventeenth century, Fez was almost taxed out of existence by the Alaouites and their leader, Moulay Ismail. Fez then began a decline that continued until the French arrived in 1912.

Under the French the old city was left intact. A new city called Ville Nouvelle was built a suitable distance away to the west and the occupants of Fez el Bali changed to the 'country poor', after its more prosperous citizens moved en mass to Ville Nouvelle.

The value of having a guide when exploring the medina cannot be overstated. We penetrate the ramparts at Bab Guissa, one of the huge wooden gates designed to repel all invaders, and commence a headlong plummet into the depths of medieval times. Rachid directs us past and into ever-narrowing and more frenetic alleyways.

The ancestors of the Andalucian and Tunisian refugee artisans are at work, oblivious to the passing, camera-toting tourists. They turn wood with the aid of their big toe guiding the chisel over the spinning wood; deftly manufacture metalwork to the din of a symphony of hammers; stitch babouches (leather slippers); tailor djellabahs; and sell all and any food that one's imagination can conjure up. Fascinating smells waft by: freshly shaved wood from the woodworkers; a mélange of spices from an alley; the chicken souk causes an immediate desire to flee; the wood-fired communal bakeries demand closer inspection – and the traditional working tannery is a veritable offence to the olfactory system, but a delight to all other senses.

Towards the end of the day, we drive up to the hill where the Merinid tombs lie. Here we join hundreds of locals taking advantage of the late afternoon sun as it washes golden and sets over the sprawling medina. The locals simply enjoy being out of close confines, but we sit numbed by the view and the memories of where we have been so entwined all day. JB

THE COOKING OF FEZ is reputed to be the jewel in the crown of all Morocco. The scene in a typical kitchen in Fez would not always revolve around the preparation of elaborate recipes, but when it does, this is a magical place to be. I am therefore very excited to be welcomed into the home of a family in Fez to participate in a day of cooking authentic Moroccan dishes. Let me tell you of this culinary treat.

Fatima (mother of our friend and guide, Rachid), emerges to greet us, softly swathed in a cosy velvet housecoat, her head covered in a customary scarf. Without a word of English but with warm eyes, expressive hands, and the manner of a kindly aunt, she teaches me much about her recipes and cooking methods. First Rachid is dispatched to collect the ingredients that have been ordered from long-trusted suppliers. He returns, laden with provisions, to amiably help with translation from time to time but otherwise to keep his distance, as cooking is definitely considered to be women's work.

We gather in Fatima's honest, practical kitchen, which is already warm and steamy with initial preparations. We plan to make several dishes, and spread ingredients out over every work surface, including what appears to be a flimsy metal filing cabinet but to my surprise turns out to be a type of gas-fired oven on legs. We are helped by Fatima's friend (also called Fatima), a charmingly capable and energetic woman with an infectious smile. Fatima is the daughter of one of Fez's out-standing wedding caterers and has generously agreed to help the older Fatima show me the secrets of some of Morocco's most famous foods.

At the top of our list is b'stilla (pronounced pasteeya) – an extraordinary type of sweet-savoury chicken pie, encased in wharka, a special type of feather-light pastry. This dish is the pride of the Moroccan kitchen. Authentically made with pigeons (though chicken makes a very acceptable substitute), b'stilla is time-consuming and elaborate and so is usually only prepared for special occasions or for entertaining distinguished guests. Moroccans rapturously describe b'stilla as 'food for the Gods'. And we are in the right town to learn the mysteries of this dish, as b'stilla from Fez is recognised as the most impressive in the country.

The Fatimas work skilfully from memory and without precise measurements, in the way that natural cooks do, following a type of inherited experience or culinary sign language. They explain their own innovations with their hands and facial gestures, and I record their methods on paper for, what they tell me, is the first time.

Fatima begins by demonstrating how the traditional, paper-thin pastry leaves of wharka are made. I am utterly captivated and amazed by this curious process that results in a very different pastry to any other I have ever known. With deft hands, flour and water are mixed into a wet dough. A fistful of dough is dabbed over a hot dry pan, just long enough for a thin film to adhere and set into a crisp sheet that is peeled off and laid on a clean tea towel. This process is repeated until an accumulation of cooked wharka pastry leaves, as light and fine as tissue paper, wait on the bench in readiness for the b'stilla's composition.

Meanwhile, the aromatic sweet-savoury filling ingredients are prepared: spiced shredded chicken bound with scrambled eggs, and fried almonds pulverised with sugar. Layers of filling are blanketed in wharka then baked (in this case, in the unique metal filing cabinet oven), until crisp and golden. To finish, the outer crust is generously dusted with icing sugar and decorated with an intricate lattice of ground cinnamon.

I now understand why this masterpiece – a true labour of love – is reserved for special guests. At the end of the day we leave the kitchen and join the family to sit at a low table in a formal room lined with colourful padded banquettes, and share the meal that we have prepared. As we communally plunge our hands into the brittle layers of pastry to unveil the warm fragrant contents, I feel thrilled to have played a part in the creation of this most magnificent b'stilla. JLEC

b'stilla

B'STILLA (PRONOUNCED PASTEEYA) IS A DISH FOR SPECIAL OCCASIONS AND IS OFTEN SERVED TO HONOUR GUESTS OR FRIENDS WHO HAVE COME TO STAY FROM ANOTHER CITY. OFTEN THE FILLING IS MADE IN PARTS IN ADVANCE AND ASSEMBLED THE NEXT DAY. THE PASTRY FOR B'STILLA IS UNUSUAL IN THAT IT IS COOKED BEFORE YOU ASSEMBLE THE PIE. THIS IS HOW YOU MAKE IT.

wharka - special b'stilla pastry

THIS IS THE AUTHENTIC WAY TO MAKE THE PASTRY FOR THIS TRADITIONAL MOROCCAN PIE AND IS AN INTRIGUING PROCESS TO FOLLOW FOR THOSE WHO HAVE THE TIME TO ENJOY NEW CULINARY CHALLENGES. HAVING SAID THIS, EVEN MOROCCAN COOKS WILL PURCHASE WHARKA FROM TRUSTED SPECIALIST MAKERS. FILO PASTRY MAKES AN ACCEPTABLE ALTERNATIVE IF DESIRED.

500g plain flour
pinch salt
enough water to mix to a wet dough
sunflower oil

1 Place flour in a bowl with salt. Add water and mix by hand to combine into a malleable, wet dough. Knead by way of slapping with the palm of your hand against the dough for 5 minutes.

2 Place a large non-stick frying pan over a large pan of simmering water. Take a handful of dough and pat this over the surface of the hot pan to lightly cover in a paper-thin film. Leave to cook for 1–2 minutes to set, then remove the sheet of pastry to a tea towel, brushing each sheet lightly with a little sunflower oil.

3 Repeat this process until many sheets of pastry have been made.

MAKES 500G WHARKA (PASTRY LEAVES) OR SUBSTITUTE 375G PACKET OF FILO PASTRY

fatima's chicken b'stilla filling

A MEDIEVAL MIXTURE OF POUNDED PIGEON, ALMONDS AND EGGS IS THE TRADITIONAL FILLING FOR B'STILLA. TODAY CHICKEN IS COMMONLY SUBSTITUTED FOR THE PIGEON.

1.4kg free-range chicken, jointed

500g red onions, peeled and chopped

1/4 cup chopped fresh parsley

1/4 cup chopped fresh coriander

1/2 teaspoon black pepper

1/2 teaspoon ground turmeric

1 teaspoon ground ginger

1/4 cup olive oil

50g butter

1/2 teaspoon salt

2 cups cold water

8 eggs, beaten

1/2 cup sugar

400g blanched almonds, toasted and ground

1 teaspoon ground cinnamon

olive oil to brush pastry layers

icing sugar and extra ground cinnamon for decoration

1   Place chicken in a large saucepan and cover with remaining ingredients, except eggs, sugar, almonds and cinnamon. Bring to the boil, then turn down the heat, cover saucepan and simmer for 1 hour.

2   Remove chicken to one side and reserve liquid. Once cool enough to handle, remove chicken meat from bones. Discard bones; shred meat and set aside.

3   Return cooking liquid to the saucepan and boil until reduced to about a cupful. Stir in beaten eggs and half the sugar and cook over a gentle heat, stirring continuously until eggs are scrambled. Adjust seasoning to taste. Strain off any excess liquid and reserve. In a bowl, combine ground almonds with remaining sugar and cinnamon.

4   Preheat oven to 200°C. To construct the b'stilla, brush a large, flat pan with oil. Layer and overlap leaves of wharka or at least 10–12 sheets of filo pastry to cover base and leave an overhang well up the sides of the pan, brushing lightly with a little oil between layers. Spread a layer of egg mixture in the base, then a layer of shredded chicken followed by a layer of almonds and a sprinkling of the reserved liquid to moisten the filling. Alternate layers until all the filling mixture has been used.

5   Fold in the overhanging edges of pastry to secure the filling. Layer remaining leaves of pastry over the top of the pie to cover filling and tuck the ends in under the bulk of the pie (like making a bed) to secure the filling, brushing with a little oil to bind layers.

6   Bake for 30–40 minutes or until pastry is golden brown and crisp. Decorate surface with a dusting of icing sugar and a lattice pattern of ground cinnamon.

SERVES 12

sweet b'stilla with almond milk

THIS LAVISH DESSERT IS LEGENDARY. THROUGHOUT MOROCCO SWEET B'STILLA IS MOST LIKELY TO BE FOUND ON THE MENUS OF EXPENSIVE RESTAURANTS, WHICH IS A SHAME BECAUSE THIS WHIMSICAL DISH IS RELATIVELY SIMPLE TO CREATE AND COMPLETELY EXQUISITE TO EAT.

1/2 cup whole blanched almonds, lightly toasted

1 tablespoon caster sugar

1/2 teaspoon cinnamon

2 sheets filo pastry

10g butter, melted

1   Preheat oven to 200°C. Place almonds, sugar and cinnamon in the bowl of a food processor and grind finely.

2   Lay 1 sheet of filo on a work surface and lightly brush with melted butter. Place second sheet of filo on top. Take a 10cm pastry cutter and cut 6 circles from the filo.

3   Brush each circle of filo with a little butter. Place the circles on a baking tray and sprinkle over the ground almond mixture to evenly cover the circles.

4   Bake for 5–10 minutes or until the circles are golden brown and crisp. Serve in a stack with almond milk as a sauce to moisten the brittle leaves of pastry.

SERVES 1

almond milk

ALMOND MILK CAN BE ENJOYED AS A DELICIOUSLY REFRESHING DRINK. OR, IT CAN BE SLIGHTLY THICKENED AND USED AS A PERFUMED SAUCE TO SOFTEN THE CRISP LAYERS OF SWEET B'STILLA.

1 cup blanched almonds

2 cups cold water

1 cup sugar

1 tablespoon cornflour dissolved in 1/4 cup milk (optional)

1 teaspoon orange flower water

1   Grind almonds in a food processor. Add 1 cup of measured water and process until smooth. Set aside.

2   Place remaining water and the sugar in a saucepan and bring to the boil, stirring until the sugar dissolves. Simmer for 5 minutes to form a syrup. Strain the almond mixture through a sieve lined with sterilised muslin; discard the almond meal. Add almond liquid to the pan; simmer for 5 minutes.

3   To form a sauce, add the cornflour dissolved in milk and stir over the heat until the mixture thickens. To make a more liquid, refreshing drink, omit this step.

4   Transfer drink or sauce to a bowl to cool, then stir in orange flower water. Chill thoroughly before serving.

SERVES 4

seafood b'stilla

SEAFOOD IS NOT A TRADITIONAL FILLING FOR B'STILLA, THOUGH OUR FRIEND FATIMA TOLD US THAT MANY MOROCCANS ARE NOW EMBRACING THE USE OF MODERN FILLINGS SUCH AS THIS.

2 tablespoons olive oil

2 large onions, finely diced

1 teaspoon paprika

400g can tomatoes, chopped

500g firm white-fleshed fish fillets, cut into 2cm cubes

1 cup shrimps or small prawns, shells removed and deveined

1/4 cup chopped fresh coriander

sea salt and freshly ground black pepper

12 sheets filo pastry

olive oil to brush tins and pastry

1 Heat a large pan, add oil and onions to cook over a moderate heat for 10 minutes until softened but not coloured. Add paprika and cook for 1 minute. Add tomatoes and simmer for 10 minutes to reduce liquid, and until sauce is thick and dry. Add fish, shrimps or prawns and coriander and cook for 5 minutes, stirring until the fish begins to break up. Season with salt and pepper to taste and set aside to cool.

2 Preheat oven to 200°C. Brush 6 10cm individual pie tins with oil. Cut 3 15x15cm squares from each sheet of filo pastry, and reserve any trimmings. Lightly oil and layer 6 squares of filo on top of each other and press these into the base of a pie tin. Repeat with remaining filo squares to line all the pie tins.

3 Spoon filling into prepared pie bases. Brush filo trimmings lightly with oil, scrunch up and use to cover surface of pies.

4 Bake for 20–25 minutes or until pastry is golden brown and crisp.

MAKES 6 INDIVIDUAL PIES

mint tea

The sharing of mint tea is a warm expression of traditional Moroccan hospitality. Mint tea is embraced as the national drink, and it is one of the true and constant pleasures of travelling in Morocco. Hosts would never dream of not offering mint tea to a guest and, likewise, it is considered bad manners for guests to refuse this gesture.

Mint tea is for drinking at any time of the day or night. This sweet fragrant nectar can be sipped in the cool shadows of an ornately tiled courtyard, sheltering from the midday sun; or in the evening, maybe in a leafy garden where fountains play and perfumed roses or orange blossoms float in small pools. Shopkeepers will pause negotiations to drink a glass or two of mint tea with a customer. Dainty glasses of steaming tea mysteriously appear at the shop, having been brought there by special tea porters. And after a meal, hot mint tea is drunk as a digestive, to delicately soothe the stomach.

The art of making Moroccan mint tea is steeped in ritual. It is a composed, deliberate and charming process that can take a good length of time. The following steps are a guide but there are no exact rules, and each tea maker will add their own personal variations to the performance.

The pot must be warmed by rinsing and swirling with boiling water at least once. Green tea leaves, mint and sugar are added to the pot in this same order, dispensed from ornate, lidded storage vessels. To be truly authentic and to create a more cohesive brew, sugar is added to the teapot rather than to the individual cups. In Morocco, sugar is usually evocatively broken from a sugar cane loaf or from attractively shaped 'sugar cones' that can be found, wrapped in coloured tissue paper, in any souk. Don't be tempted to skimp on the addition of sugar, as too little will produce a bitter brew – and it is believed that sharing sweet tea demonstrates generosity. JLEC.

moroccan mint tea

THERE ARE NO TRULY MEASURABLE PROPORTIONS FOR MAKING PERFECT MINT TEA. MUCH IS LEFT TO PERSONAL PREFERENCE AND THE QUALITY OF THE INGREDIENTS. ADAPT THIS RECIPE TO YOUR OWN TASTE AND BE AWARE THAT NO TWO MIXTURES WILL EVER TASTE THE SAME.

1 teaspoon Chinese gunpowder or green tea leaves per person

several good sprigs of fresh mint or spearmint

2 sugar lumps or 2 teaspoons sugar per person, at least, or more to taste

1 cup boiling water

1 The ritual begins: warm the teapot by rinsing once or twice with boiling water. Place the tea leaves, mint and sugar in the teapot.

2 Pour over boiling water to cover and leave to steep for some minutes.

3 Pour one glass of tea, then pour this back into the pot (to mix). Taste a little tea to test whether more sugar is required.

4 Pour tea from a height (to aerate the brew) into a small decorative glass, sip and be transported to fragrant Morocco.

SERVES 1

animals of morocco

Our car was the only one to screech to a halt at the sight of a herd of goats calmly grazing up in the branches of a grove of Argan trees. Sheep, goats, a camel yoked to a cow as it pulls a plough, and an ass plodding a weary circle around an ancient olive press are all as much a part of the everyday Moroccan scenery as the ubiquitous donkey carrying produce to market. JB

midelt

MIDELT IS DESTINED TO APPEAR INSIGNIFICANT, squatting as it does in the middle of a vast valley between the Middle Atlas, High Atlas and Jbel Ayachi mountain ranges. Situated deep within the Moroccan interior and having an altitude of 1500 metres, it has a climate of extremes: devilishly hot and dusty in summer, bitterly cold and wind-blown in winter. Despite the apparent barrenness of the area, apples and stone fruit are grown in profusion within densely cultivated orchards.

With a need for dinner we venture into a restaurant, and half the town comes to watch. They alternate their gaze between us and a wall-sized television, which is playing, for a reason that no one could explain, movies in English. The only table troubling the haik-adorned female cook is our own. The locals studiously occupy themselves with repeated glasses of Berber 'whisky', a gumboot tea infused with absinthe. One could argue that this mildly narcotic beverage is an agreeably inventive way around Islam's prohibition of alcohol.

The atmosphere at our hotel is livelier when we return. Traditional Berber music is blasting from the bar but the only musical instrument in evidence is a Moroccan version of a violin, one string but bowed like a cello. Boisterous percussion accompaniment is provided by the bar patrons with anything that makes sound. An upturned pot added bass; table-tops, knee-slapping, the tapping of empty bottles and clapping provides a deafening rhythm. Vocals are led by a somewhat scruffy chap whose prowess and respect has clearly been established with the crowd. The music, at first cacophonous, soon becomes thoroughly hypnotic. Only the prospect of the next day being equally exhilarating forces us to bed.

A typical tourist outing is to drive from Fez to either Erfoud or Marrakech in one day. If time is limited and one has the patience to sit for eight or so hours, then this is certainly one way to see the country. The downside of this strategy is the loss of many opportunities to partake of the real and unspoiled Morocco. To travel independently, and therefore have more time, offers the reward of being able to stop whenever a sight takes your interest.

The high plateaux of the Middle Atlas are one of the world's true wonders. The sheering multi-tectonic forces of long ago have created a voluptuous backdrop of striated, twisted and coloured mountain faces. They enclose the gently undulating, tussocked valleys, all under the deepest blue Moroccan sky. Other than the occasional traditionally garbed shepherd, wearing layers of muted djellabahs to ward off the mountain cold and guarding their small flocks of hardy sheep, there is little sign of human habitation over our two-hour drive.

But even in the midst of nowhere, there are interludes of interest that divert from the landscape's breathtaking visual feast. Beside a braided wadi, five camels take turns to rub themselves, their lips curled in pleasure, on a solitary sign warning motorists to be watchful for wandering cattle. An old woman motivates her firewood-laden donkey with a thin bent stick. The mere sighting of the camera spurs her and her donkey into a canter.

South of Midelt, towards the widest part of the plateaux, a brown smudge in the distance gradually materialises into a tented Berber dwelling. The kilometre or so walk from the roadside reveals that the tent is a collection of roughly woven wool materials, fastened more by gravity than anything else. Inside, the contents amount to nothing more than a ground cover of old woollen rugs and a small pile of cloth bags that hold the family's few possessions. This is a scene of life in the raw. Overnight the temperature has hovered around 0°C, and even at 10 a.m. it hasn't risen much more. While the children are asserting their need for pens (and if we don't have any, then money will do), their father is proudly introducing us individually to each of his flock of sheep and goats. They are tightly penned in a corral that has the look of having been hastily constructed from flotsam collected on their travels, along with roughly piled stones.

Alone, in the centre of the next completely deserted valley, a white horse stands tethered to an old rusting car wreck. A photo was required to prove this surreal scene. The horse obliged. JB

THE MIDDLE ATLAS IS FAMED for the authentic Berber recipe, m'choui. Today, all regions of Morocco have adopted this tantalising dish of the nomadic desert Bedouin Berbers, who have always roamed the region with family and flock.

For m'choui, a whole seasoned lamb is slow-roasted on a spit over a fire set inside a deep mud-oven pit. The lamb is first rubbed with a paste of flavourings – salt and black pepper, cumin, and sweet and hot red peppers blended with butter. The skewered whole lamb is continuously turned during its long, slow cooking time of four to five hours, and basted regularly. This age-old method results in moist, tender meat encased in a highly seasoned, almost lacquer-textured crust. The ritual preparation of this celebratory dish is generally reserved as a meal for special-occasion banquets, where it takes centre stage.

The traditional dishes of the mountain and desert Berber people are inclined to be simple and rustic because of the ingredients historically available to them. In the city, however, m'choui can be replicated in other ways. Whole lambs may be cooked in the communal baker's oven. A leg of lamb or some other joint of the animal, seasoned in the usual m'choui way, may be roasted in home ovens or possibly on a spit over a small fire lit in a courtyard reminiscent of a barbecue.

In the French tradition, Moroccans call skewered small portions of meat by the name brochette. All kinds of meat (chicken, beef, lamb and mutton) and mince (kefta) are threaded onto skewers and cooked over charcoal grills. Often pieces of fat are woven between the skewered meat to keep it moist as it browns. If you are more adventurous you might try offal that has been given this skewered treatment, such as elaborately herb-stuffed lamb or calf's livers, securely wrapped in a lacy net of caul fat. While these liver parcels can be found on some street food stalls, they are usually served as a traditional accompaniment to m'choui.

Brochettes can readily be tasted on the street, cooked and dispensed from tiny stalls or single table cafés. Simply follow the billowing smoke and enticing barbecue aromas that attract hungry passers-by to this ubiquitous street food. While you wait, long skewered chains of diminutive meat cubes will be grilled over glowing charcoal embers lining iron braziers. The burning-hot barbecued meat is then quickly and deftly stripped from the skewers and bundled into halved flatbread rounds, to be eaten like a sandwich. This way, none of the aromatic juices are lost, as they melt into the bread, making it similarly succulent and delicious.

Kefta are a form of brochette where minced meat (lamb or beef) is pounded together with seasonings until velvety in texture, then moulded onto skewers (see page 50). The resulting sausage-shaped kefta, when cooked, remains delightfully moist and fragrant with a discrete combination of spices. The same basic recipe can be used to make round meatballs, which are either cooked in a preserved lemon sauce or a tomato sauce, sometimes with the addition of poached eggs (see page 103). Like so many traditional dishes, the recipe for kefta will vary from village to village and even from person to person.

The typical Moroccan salad of finely diced tomatoes, cucumber, red onions and parsley with a tangy citrus dressing is often served on the side of brochettes, like a salsa. Ground cumin and salt are available on the table rather than salt and pepper. Or, sometimes specially blended cumin salt can be wrapped in a small cone of paper to go. Harissa, a spice-scented paste of fiery hot chillies, is another popular condiment for brochettes (see page 67).

In Morocco, brochettes are not limited to street food stalls. Throughout the land, from the finest restaurants of the Imperial Cities to rustic rural eateries, skewered foods will feature on menus. We ate fancily presented versions in smart restaurants in Marrakech, Fez and Casablanca. In a typical eatery in Midelt, we enjoyed a set menu consisting of a mixed salad starter, followed by a variety of chargrilled brochettes served with pommes frites (due to the French influence, once again). And fresh local fruits, predominantly oranges, grapes and apples provided a simple palate-cleansing dessert.

For nostalgic travellers or those dreaming of visiting this exotic land, brochettes are the easiest Moroccan street food to replicate at home. To produce an authentic smoky flavour, I recommend firing up the barbecue or simply browning the skewered food under a preheated grill. JLEC

SKEWERED MARINATED BEEF WITH CORIANDER

kefta

KEFTA ARE KEBABS OF MINCED MEAT MOULDED ONTO SKEWERS AND GRILLED OVER COALS.
POUNDING OR KNEADING THE MINCE WITH YOUR HANDS UNTIL IT IS SOFT AND PLIABLE IS AN
IMPORTANT PART OF THE PREPARATION AS THE MEAT NEEDS TO BE SMOOTH IN TEXTURE.

650g minced lamb or beef

1 small red onion, grated or very finely chopped

3 cloves garlic, crushed

1 teaspoon each ground cumin,
coriander and paprika

2 tablespoons chopped parsley

2 tablespoons olive oil

sea salt and freshly ground black pepper

1   Combine mince, onion, garlic, spices, parsley and olive oil
    in a bowl. Knead and pound well with your fist or process
    briefly in a food processor to produce a smooth mixture.
    Season with salt and pepper to taste.

2   Preheat a barbecue or a gas or electric grill. Mould mixture
    in sausage shapes onto skewers. Barbecue or grill for 2
    minutes on each side or until browned all over.

SERVES 4

aubergine brochettes with cumin salt

CUMIN SALT IS UBIQUITOUS THROUGHOUT MOROCCO. CUMIN AND SALT ARE THE CONDIMENTS OF
PREFERENCE AND APPEAR IN PLACE OF THE SALT AND BLACK PEPPER OF WESTERN TABLES.

1kg (2 large) aubergine (eggplant)

1 teaspoon ground cumin

1 teaspoon sea salt

2 cloves garlic, crushed

pinch chilli powder

1/3 cup olive oil

2 red onions, halved and then cut into four

extra cumin and salt

1   Cut the aubergine into 3cm cubes. Combine cumin, salt,
    garlic, chilli powder and olive oil in a bowl.

2   Preheat a barbecue or a gas or electric grill. Thread aubergine
    cubes onto skewers alternating with pieces of onion.

3   Brush all over with the cumin-flavoured oil mixture. Barbecue
    or grill for 2–3 minutes on each side or until browned all over.

4   Serve dusted with extra cumin salt to taste.

SERVES 4

chicken brochettes with harissa

MOROCCANS FREQUENTLY CALL THEIR STYLE OF KEBABS, BROCHETTES, IN THE FRENCH MANNER.

4 skinless chicken breasts
1 tablespoon harissa (see page 67)
3 tablespoons extra virgin olive oil
sea salt and freshly ground black pepper
mint leaves to serve

1   Cut the chicken breasts into 1cm-wide long strips. Combine the harissa and olive oil in a bowl. Add the strips of chicken and toss well. Leave to marinate for several hours or preferably overnight to tenderise and flavour the chicken.

2   Preheat a barbecue or a gas or electric grill. Thread 1 strip of chicken onto each skewer and season with salt and pepper. Barbecue or grill for 2–3 minutes on each side or until browned all over.

3   Serve on a bed of mint leaves if desired.

SERVES 4

skewered lamb with ginger and mint

THIS IS BUT ONE EXAMPLE OF A MARINADE FOR BROCHETTES. THE POSSIBILITIES FOR FLAVOURING SKEWERED MEATS ARE LIMITED ONLY BY YOUR IMAGINATION.

600g lamb shoulder steaks, trimmed of fat
2 tablespoons finely grated root ginger
1 teaspoon ground cinnamon
3 tablespoons olive oil
2 tablespoons chopped fresh mint
sea salt and freshly ground black pepper

1   Cut the lamb steaks into 1cm cubes. Place the marinade ingredients, except the salt and pepper, in a bowl. Add the meat and toss well. Leave to marinate for several hours or preferably overnight to tenderise and flavour the meat.

2   Preheat a barbecue or a gas or electric grill. Thread the meat cubes onto skewers and season with salt and pepper. Barbecue or grill for 1–2 minutes on each side or until browned all over.

SERVES 4

skewered marinated beef with coriander

THE AROMA OF MARINATED MEAT BROWNING OVER CHARCOAL BRAZIERS IS THE BEST FORM OF ADVERTISING FOR MANY A STREET VENDOR.

600g beef steak, such as sirloin or rump, trimmed of fat

2 teaspoons ground coriander

3 tablespoons olive oil

juice of 1 lemon

1/4 cup chopped fresh coriander

sea salt and freshly ground black pepper

1 Cut the steak into 1cm cubes. Place the marinade ingredients, except the salt and pepper, in a bowl. Add the meat and toss well. Leave to marinate for several hours or preferably overnight to tenderise and flavour the meat.

2 Preheat a barbecue or a gas or electric grill. Thread the meat cubes onto skewers and season with salt and pepper. Barbecue or grill for 1–2 minutes on each side or until browned all over.

SERVES 4

fish kebabs with paprika and orange

FIRM, MEATY-FLESHED FISH, SUCH AS TUNA, KINGFISH, SWORDFISH OR MONKFISH, WORK PARTICULARLY WELL THREADED ONTO SKEWERS AND MARINATED IN THIS REFRESHING MIXTURE BEFORE BEING BARBECUED OR GRILLED.

800g thick firm-fleshed fish, skin and bones removed

juice of 1 blood orange (or 1 ordinary orange)

juice of 1 lemon

3 tablespoons olive oil

1 teaspoon each paprika and ground cumin

2 cloves garlic, crushed

sea salt and freshly ground black pepper

1 Cut fish fillets into 2cm cubes and place in a bowl. Sprinkle with orange and lemon juice, oil, paprika, cumin and garlic; toss well and leave to marinate for 1 hour.

2 Preheat a barbecue or a gas or electric grill. Thread fish cubes onto skewers and season with salt and pepper. Barbecue or grill for 1–2 minutes on each side or until browned all over.

SERVES 4

spice

Spice stores are the heart of the souk; just as surely as the spices themselves form the soul of Moroccan cooking. Spices enchant Moroccan cooks in such a way that they are able to use them in clever and surprisingly subtle amounts to create magic, and even some mystery as to which spices a dish may contain. The basic ingredients of the Moroccan kitchen are essentially uncomplicated, however, with the careful addition of spices, simple dishes are expertly brought to exotic heights.

It is good to see that the wonderful tradition of multiple spice blends is still strong in Morocco. Many cooks we met during our travels spoke of their own combinations, mixtures of any-where between three to seven spices, concocted according to personal and often secret proportions. To blend your own Moroccan-inspired mix, a logical grouping might include cumin, coriander, ginger, saffron or turmeric, cinnamon, paprika, allspice, and chilli powder, combined to taste.

Of all the spice blends in the world, ras el hanout is possibly the most complicated and highly prized. Meaning 'the head of the shop', ras el hanout is an eloquent fusion of more than two dozen extraordinary spices that when combined are commonly added to certain warming winter dishes (see tagine recipe page 111), and always used in the cooking of game.

Cardamom, mace, nutmeg, various types of pepper, paprika, ginger, lavender, dried roses from the valleys of Morocco, sweet cinnamon and fennel are but a few of the more obvious ingredients of ras el hanout. Many of the strange and exotic additions, such as cantharides or Spanish fly and monk's pepper (both reputed aphrodisiacs), and also belladonna berries, are hard to find outside Morocco.

These days, few Moroccans make their own ras el hanout, preferring to leave the art of blending and grinding to a trusted purveyor. Spice shops sell either pre-ground powders or they will freshly grind raw ingredients, on demand, to their own secret recipe and proportions. This is my own personal combination from which you might like to experiment and make adjustments to suit your own taste preferences. JLEC

ras el hanout

A COMPLEX MULTIPLE-SPICE BLEND.

1 teaspoon each fennel, cumin and coriander seeds, toasted and ground

1 teaspoon each ground turmeric cinnamon

2 teaspoons each sweet paprika and ginger

1/2 teaspoon each cayenne, ground nutmeg, cloves, allspice and cardamom

1/2 teaspoon each sea salt and freshly ground black pepper

1   Combine all spices and store in a sealed jar. Because spices lose their pungency with age, blend ras el hanout in small batches, as required.

MAKES 1/4 CUP

simple moroccan spice blend

THIS LESS COMPLEX SPICE BLEND IS VERY USEFUL TO ADD TO SOUPS AND STEWS.

2 teaspoons each ground cumin, coriander, paprika, ginger and cinnamon

1 teaspoon each ground white pepper and turmeric

1/4 teaspoon each chilli powder and ground nutmeg

1   Combine all spices and stored in a sealed jar.

MAKES 1/4 CUP

the humble donkey

These frequently encountered creatures are beguiling, whether they are toiling up a narrow alley with a heavy load or just idly tethered in a souk or field. Their gentle persona exudes loyalty. Many of the 800,000 donkeys in Morocco, and in particular those working in the medinas, have muzzles made of plastic containers. They are not to stop them biting, spitting or giving you a quick lick, but merely to prevent the donkeys from nicking fruit from the stalls in the narrow lanes as they pass on their endless rounds. JB

erfoud

ERFOUD WAS NAMED by the Alawiti tribe after they rode in from the Sahara in the fourteenth century. The French saw no need to change the name although they did transform Erfoud into a garrison town. It is now a Berber encampment, languorous and still. In spite of the French presence, the staunchly independent locals made sure they were one of the last areas of southern Morocco to capitulate rule, while reserving their future right to reign. To this day, apart from the period of the French occupation, the descendants of these hardy, horse-riding Berbers from the Sahara have ruled Morocco for over 350 years.

Tourists adopting Erfoud as a base for outings to the Sahara's edge have lately breathed life into this town. While Erfoud is sand-coloured, sand-covered, and, when an easterly wind blows, sand-blasted, it exudes a 'wild west' charm that is a perfect introduction to Erg Chebbi, a massive Saharan sand dune to its south-east.

The time that it takes to get to Erg Chebbi depends on your driver's desire to live. Merzouga, the town at the bottom of the dune, is approximately thirty minutes' drive from Erfoud. The last ten minutes of the journey are spent rattling along the corrugated tracks of an eerily flat pisé, littered with black stones. The mountainous sand dunes don't seem to be getting any closer, despite the fact that our car is hurtling towards them.

Covered in dust, we pull up at the base of the Everest-like Erg Chebbi. With legs, arms and camera gear flailing (in an effort to beat sundown), we quickly discover that running on the sand of the rippled, sharp-angled sides of the lower slopes is not easy. Breathless by now, we longingly gaze at the camel trains, laden with inactive passengers, gently ambulating up the north face of what is reputed to be the tallest sand dune in Morocco. The closing distance to the camels and their blue-cloaked Berber guides, etched black against the cloudless, royal blue, North African sky draws us on.

Closer to sunset, the dunes turn tangerine orange before rapidly blurring to red. As the sand smudges with the darkening of night, a clear, white full moon rises stage left, heralding the second act of this daily performance. Dragging the eyes 180 degrees from the declining light show, reveals that the sunset in the far distance is now in full bloom, gushing every hue of red over the Middle Atlas Mountains.

Solitude pervades all. Once both light shows have finally dimmed,

we are overwhelmed by a sense of being well and truly in the middle of an ancient land, only thirty kilometres from Morocco's eastern border and about as close as anyone can get to Algeria and the rest of the Sahara. Sitting in near dark, one cannot help but reflect on the Berber poem we read during the drive:

> We, the men of the caravans,
> Have only the sky and the sands
> But after the heat of the day
> There comes the call of the night
> So why should we complain?

Those who don't want to undertake the trip up the dunes sit contently on the rooftops of hotels dotted for many miles along the dune's edge, enjoying a mezze plate and a cool drink. In the sand alongside the hotels, colourful and traditionally basic Berber tents emit the sound of thumping generators; a stark contrast to the solitude that has just been experienced on top of the Sahara.

Visitors intent on experiencing Morocco's only genuine sand dune could easily remain blissfully unaware that the souk in the centre of town is refreshingly uninhabited and largely untainted by tourism. A surprising number of shopkeepers here speak English as a result, no doubt, of taking eager tourists into the desert to supplement their income.

Seeing the dunes is justification enough; getting to Erfoud is another treat altogether. The northern access route into Erfoud hugs the Ziz River as it meanders the length of the Tafilalet Valley, down deep gullies and gorges, before dissipating into a sandy grave on reaching the sponge-like Sahara. We pass hundreds of mud-plastered houses; like chameleons they blend into the striated hillside. The bright, white-framed windows and colourful clothing and bedding around the houses drying on the warm rocks are the only exceptions to the earthy tones.

From the depths of the gorge, donkeys carry Herculean loads of reeds, zigzagging well-trodden tracks to the fortified villages, called kasars, hanging high above the river. At the centre of the kasars, storks have built nests that mushroom from the top of the minarets of each mosque. The pure white of the stork chicks are the only relief against the Moroccan blue sky. The kasars themselves are a tangled concentration of tightly bunched abodes, squeezed into the few square metres of arable land not devoted to growing date palms. JB

A FRENETIC THEATRE OF NOISE, movement and riotous colour all but blocks the road. The cause of the heightened activity in this small rural village of El Broj, just outside the town of Erfoud, is the local weekly souk. Progress is slow through the organised whirl of products and people; eventually coming to a standstill becomes a necessity. This stop, however, turns out to be fortuitous, as the chance to be involved in this actively unfolding scene is compelling.

The street is teeming with donkeys and carts, ancient bicycles, proud local men dressed in traditional hooded djellabahs, giggling clusters of children on their way to school, and women enveloped in flowing black haiks. Splashes of vivid colour can be glimpsed from beneath these black veils as the women go about their weekly shopping – shocking pink, parrot green, pumpkin, azure blue, vermilion and teal; a kaleidoscope that indirectly hints at another side to their lives.

Like all souks, even this provincial roadside market is divided into sections. The clothing section flows into hardware, which in turn flows into the area reserved for household goods and kitchenalia. On display, all jumbled together, are rows of omnipresent teapots, every kind of kitchen utensil, various sieves for making couscous or for baking, stacks of pots and pans, tagines and local ceramics.

In one corner of this scene lies the donkey park (taking the place of a car park), where these humble workers are tethered while their owners look around or make purchases. Close by, men gather to inspect and bargain over an assorted collection of goats and sheep, and what appears to be a donkey auction is in progress. On the periphery of this accumulation of live-stock, straw-lined baskets of eggs and a huddle of live chickens are placed for sale.

Food products, naturally, cover a large section of the souk. On the ground in a small clearing, deep hand-woven baskets and brightly coloured plastic buckets display pyramids of recently harvested olives or heaps of fresh dates. Couscous is presented piled high in flat baskets, and sacks overflow with dried beans, lentils and other grains. Locally grown artichoke stalks, irresistibly ripe tomatoes, fat garlic bulbs, bunches of carrots tied up with string, and fresh fava (broad) beans are plentiful. These vegetables are spread out over blue canvas sheets on the ground, along with great perfumed bunches of mint and hampers of absinthe – important ingredients for the making of Berber tea.

At this particular souk, it is the dates that most fascinate me. Date palms, one of the world's oldest fruit trees, grow in profusion in irrigated oases not far from here. Rows of veiled women sit beside their baskets and buckets of dates. The women shyly pull their haiks around themselves so that only one eye is showing, and yet their inquisitive smiles are still visibly percep-tible. They offer many different varieties of dates for sale, making a taste test necessary to determine which type is best for eating and which is more suitable for cooking. Some dates are intensely sticky and sweet; others are more firm and chewy; and certain varieties have a crunchy, almost watery texture.

Moroccans will eat this naturally sweet and pliable amber-coloured fruit fresh as a snack with several glasses of hot mint tea. One of the most obvious culinary uses for this fruit is in the making of traditional sweets and pastries, many of which contain a luscious, sticky date filling. Moroccans also have a particular penchant for marrying dates with meat in rich savoury tagines.

The intoxicating scent of spices saturates the air and entices purchasers in yet another direction – the spice sellers can be found along the roadside nestled under makeshift awnings, protected from the penetrating sun. A long list of spices plays a central and meaningful part in local cooking, and so the spice stalls always form one of the busiest sections of the souk.

Conical mounds of colourful and pungent powders burst from large tin canisters. Baskets bulge with an assortment of intriguing seeds, twisted sticks and bark. It is here that animated discussions take place. Small amounts of freshly ground spices are scooped and weighed and wrapped in cones of paper; money changes hands. The small parcels disappear under a haik and another cook leaves with exotic inspiration in her pocket. Here in the countryside, where basic cooking ingredi-ents are sometimes few, locals work with an imaginative use of spices to bring simple dishes together in a way that is ornate with fragrance and flavour.

It is hard to withdraw from this dynamic culinary arena. As we pull ourselves away and depart along the road, women are also leaving, carrying enormous bundles of shopping on their heads in the traditional African fashion. Men pass on bicycles with sheaths of mint tucked around the handlebars, and blanketed donkeys tug small carts laden with their owner's assorted pur-chases. We leave with the strong impression that within this vibrancy lies the true essence of Morocco. JLEC

spiced aubergine

THIS VOLUPTUOUS AUBERGINE DISH CAN BE SERVED AS A DIP OR SPREAD WITH FLATBREAD, OR AS A SALAD OR SIDE DISH FOR MEATS.

1kg (2 large) aubergine (eggplant)

1/4 cup olive oil

3 cloves garlic, chopped

2 teaspoons paprika

1 teaspoon ground cumin, toasted

1/4 teaspoon harissa (see page 67) or chilli powder

1/2 cup cold water

2 tablespoons olive oil

juice of 2 lemons

sea salt and freshly ground black pepper

1   Preheat oven to 170°C. Cut aubergine into 1cm-thick slices. Brush slices on both sides with olive oil and place in a single layer on a baking tray lined with non-stick baking paper. Bake for 20–30 minutes, turning once, until aubergine slices have softened and turned golden brown.

2   Roughly chop aubergine slices and transfer to a bowl. Add garlic, spices and water and mix well.

3   Heat 2 tablespoons olive oil in a frying pan, add the mashed eggplant mixture and cook over a gentle heat for 10 minutes or until the moisture has evaporated and mixture is thick and jam-like. Add lemon juice and cook for 1–2 minutes more. Season with salt and pepper to taste.

4   Spiced aubergine will last for 3–4 days, stored in the fridge. Bring to room temperature before serving with bread or as a side dish.

SERVES 6

carrot and harissa purée

THIS PURÉE IS WONDERFULLY VERSATILE — YOU CAN SERVE IT COLD AS A DIP OR MEZZE, OR HOT AS A VEGETABLE ACCOMPANIMENT. I PARTICULARLY LIKE TO EAT IT AS A SALAD AND FIND THAT THE PURÉE FORMS A DELICIOUSLY THICK, DRESSING-LIKE ADDITION TO A MIXED SALAD.

700g (4 large) carrots, peeled and roughly chopped

2 cloves garlic, peeled and roughly chopped

1/3 cup extra virgin olive oil

1 teaspoon harissa (see below)

sea salt and freshly ground black pepper

1   Cook carrots in boiling salted water until tender. Drain well and while still warm process with garlic in a food processor, adding oil to work into a smooth and creamy paste.

2   Add harissa and process to blend. Season with salt and pepper to taste.

MAKES ABOUT 2 CUPS

harissa

ORIGINATING IN TUNISIA BUT COMMON TO THE COUNTRIES OF THE MAGHREB, HARISSA IS A FIERY HOT CHILLI PASTE BOUND WITH SPICES AND OLIVE OIL. THIS IS ONE OF THE MANY POSSIBLE VERSIONS OF THIS CONDIMENT, WHICH SHOULD BE THICK IN CONSISTENCY.

1 cup dried red chillies, stems removed

3 cloves garlic, peeled

1/2 teaspoon sea salt

1 teaspoon cumin seeds, toasted and ground

1 tablespoon olive oil

1   Cover dried chillies with boiling water and leave to soak for 1 hour. Strain off water and roughly chop chillies.

2   Pound chillies together with remaining ingredients in a mortar and pestle or food processor until a thick paste is formed.

3   Store in the refrigerator covered with a film of oil. Use only in small amounts, as harissa is a powerfully hot and potently flavoured condiment.

MAKES 1/2 CUP

olives

The olive section is tucked into a small square of its own within the great souk of Marrakech. Turning in from a dusty alleyway and stumbling upon this extraordinary display causes a sense of amazement time and again. A veritable profusion of plump olives piled high in huge enamel bowls have been intricately arranged in conical formations. The symphony of colour is astounding, as the olives range in hue from bright green, dusky pink, violet and pale brown to deep red, purple and opulent black. To be able to appreciate the variety of flavours that olives reveal, they really must be tasted. In the heat of the day, the briny buttery flesh sparkles and melts in the mouth. Vendors will proudly present you with an enticing sample or three to make a taste comparison.

Around the edge of the stalls, display jars contain more olives in various other guises. Green olives are neatly stuffed with pimiento or bathed in a vibrant herbal marinade and packed into tall glass jars. The Moroccans' masterful use of spices is put to work in a marinade for black olives, blending fiery harissa or an array of aromatics with olive oil and preserved lemon. Watchful stall-holders constantly attend to their wares and tidy the arrangements as they are ravaged, polishing the pyramids of olives with oil so that they glisten enticingly like jewels. JLEC

chermoula

CHERMOULA MAKES A GREAT DIPPING SAUCE FOR FLATBREAD, HOWEVER, THIS WET SPICE MIX IS TRADITIONALLY USED AS A MARINADE, ESPECIALLY FOR FISH.

1 bunch fresh coriander or parsley

3 cloves garlic, peeled

1 teaspoon each ground cumin, coriander and paprika

1 small red chilli, seeds removed

1/2 teaspoon sea salt

juice of 1 lemon

1/4 cup olive oil

1 Pound all ingredients together in a mortar and pestle or food processor to form a rough-textured paste.

2 Chermoula can be stored in the refrigerator for 2–3 days.

MAKES ABOUT 1 CUP

marinated olives

I'VE TASTED MANY DIFFERENT VERSIONS OF MARINATED OLIVES FROM SOUKS ALL OVER MOROCCO. THIS IS ONE OF MY FAVOURITE COMBINATIONS – THOUGH I HAVE TO POINT OUT THAT OLIVES TOSSED IN CHERMOULA (ABOVE) IS ANOTHER GREAT MOROCCAN TASTE SENSATION.

1 cup black olives

1 cup green olives or small olives for contrast

finely grated zest of 2 lemons

3 cloves garlic, peeled and sliced

2 tablespoons chopped fresh coriander

2 red chillies, seeds removed, sliced

1 teaspoon toasted fennel seeds

extra virgin olive oil, to cover olives

1 Drain and dry olives. Make a slit in each olive (or roughly crush olives with a rolling pin) to help the olives absorb the flavours of the marinade.

2 Combine olives with marinade ingredients and toss well. Cover with plastic wrap and leave to marinate for 24 hours at room temperature. Store in the refrigerator; use within a month.

3 Drain olives from excess oil to serve. This flavoured oil can be used in dressings.

MAKES 2 CUPS

tomato jam

TOMATO JAM CAN BE EATEN COLD AS PART OF A GROUP OF MEZZE DISHES. OR, I FIND THAT IT MAKES A DELICIOUS SAUCE FOR SIMPLY GRILLED MEATS OR CHICKEN. EITHER WAY, THIS PERFUMED TOMATO MIXTURE MUST BE REDUCED UNTIL IT IS INCREDIBLY THICK AND JAM-LIKE.

3 tablespoons olive oil

1 onion, peeled and finely diced

pinch saffron threads

1/2 teaspoon each ground ginger and cinnamon

2 x 400g cans tomatoes, roughly chopped

1/4 cup honey

sea salt and freshly ground black pepper

1　Heat a saucepan, add oil and onion and cook over a moderate heat for 10 minutes to soften but not colour. Add saffron, ginger and cinnamon and cook for 1 minute.

2　Add tomatoes and honey and bring to the boil. Turn down the heat and simmer gently, stirring regularly, for 30–40 minutes or until any excess liquid has evaporated and the tomato mixture is very thick and jam-like.

3　Season with salt and pepper to taste. Remove to cool and serve at room temperature as a dip or spread for bread, or as a condiment for grilled meats.

MAKES 3 CUPS

potato crisps

VENDORS, WHO ROAM THE SOUKS PUSHING HANDCARTS, DISPENSE THESE PAPER-THIN CRISPS PILED HIGH INTO PAPER CONES AND LIBERALLY SALTED. THIS SIMPLE STREET FOOD, WHICH LITERALLY COSTS NEXT TO NOTHING, MAKES A GREAT SNACK TO NIBBLE WHILE BROWSING THE STALLS.

4 medium-sized all-purpose potatoes, peeled

2 litres olive or sunflower oil for frying

sea salt

1　Cut potatoes into very fine slices – use a special mandolin for best effect, or be patient and use a very sharp knife. Rinse the potato slices to remove excess starch, then pat dry on paper towels. Be sure to dry well because any moisture will cause the oil to dangerously splatter during cooking.

2　Place oil in a large saucepan and heat to 180°C or test by adding a small piece of bread to the oil – if the oil is at the correct temperature, the bread will float to the surface of the hot oil and sizzle to a golden brown.

3　Fry dried potato slices in batches until golden brown. Remove to drain on paper towels. Sprinkle with salt to serve.

SERVES 6

OUARZAZATE IS THE PERFECT STAGING POINT for great adventures in the Draa and Dadès valleys that lie to the east of this youthful town. Ouarzazate was established by the French in the 1920s to quell rebellious Berber tribes of the south and has of late centred its attention on catering to the needs of tourists and the film industry.

The relative youth of Ouarzazate shows in wide roads, the use of concrete instead of rammed earth, and plenty of hotels of every star rating. On the outskirts of town, a vast area is being converted into a grand film studio. If size is an indication of potential, watch out Hollywood. Hundreds of films have had the Ouarzazate area as their setting, most famously *Lawrence of Arabia*, filmed nearby in Ait-Benhaddou.

On first sighting of Ouarzazate, there is little traditionally Moroccan to entice the visitor. However, a pleasant hour or so can be spent by delving into the old medina. This medina is hidden behind the tourist shops in the Centre Artisanal and beside Ouarzazate's only historical building, the Taorirt Kasbah. The medina is very authentic although not particularly salubrious. The locals may be somewhat surprised to see you and this may result in some interesting conversation and interaction. On the other hand, the Taorirt Kasbah was once truly grand but is now badly in need of restoration. Once one of the largest kasbahs in Morocco, it was built by the Glaoui clan as an integral part of their expansionist control of the south. The Glaouis were formidable warriors and their leader, Thami El Glaoui, an astute politician and leader, is perhaps better known as the Pasha of Marrakech. This title came as a result of the French rewarding him with control of most of southern Morocco in exchange for his continuing loyalty. His actions were fundamental in Mohammed V's return from exile; his demise and Morocco's independence from France followed soon after.

The journey from Ouarzazate to Marrakech provides a full and enthralling day's drive. Just a short detour off the main highway to the west are the sprawling kasbahs of Ait-Benhaddou. From a distance it appears be a single structure, but as you get closer you realise it is a tight cluster of buildings, built cheek by jowl and composed entirely of the rich red surrounding soil,

rammed upright and blending subtly into the hillside on which it appears to drape. Were it not for the shadows cast by its crenulated parapets and towers, the buildings would all but disappear in the bright sunlight. Come sunset, the red buildings pulse with the added orange and red hues of the day's gently fading light. At the base of the hill, a shallow crystal-clear river meanders through the flat and fertile valley on which crops are tended and animals graze. Marvellous!

UNESCO selected Ait-Benhaddou as a world heritage site in 1994. Within the kasbahs, only a handful of families reside, alongside approximately a hundred shops offering a colourful array of products and services. In addition, the government's restoration of the entire area has spurred the building of a new village and entry point on a hilltop on the other side of the river, catering to the needs of countless visitors.

This area is a haven for fossil buyers. The Tizi-n-Tichka and Tizi-n-Ait-Imguer mountain passes twist across the High Atlas mountain range. These high-altitude passes and the flamboyant attention-grabbing actions of the fossil stall-owners are impossible to avoid because there is only one vaguely direct road between Ouarzazate and Marrakech. There are more fossil shops than bends in the road, and just stopping the car is a signal to some distant boy to scamper up a vertical hillside and display his stock. You may not buy anything but you have to admire the location of each stall. Stalls are often found clinging to the outside bend of a tight corner. Looking over the stock, carefully balanced on the rock-walled crash barriers, there is a drop of thousands of feet, providing the most glorious panoramic views into the valleys scything through the mountainous terrain.

The final leg of the journey to Marrakech is a fifty-kilometre dash across a richly cultivated plain. Suddenly, the vista becomes green and manicured. Olive trees rake regimentally back from the road and glistening piles of freshly picked olives are mounded roadside, ready for collection by truck and delivery to the presses. Such is Morocco that in the space of only a few hours we have left the Sahara hinterland behind and have arrived again in the land of plenty. JB

RED MUD-BRICK HOUSES BLEND INTO yet also rise from the same coloured earth. We pass through extraordinary scenes of once great, now crumbling adobe kasbahs; desert and camel picture-postcard images; desperately poor and barren villages in contrast to neighbouring lush green oases filled with date palms and other patches of fertile agricultural land.

It is spring and the almond trees are bursting with delicate petals in the palest shade of pink. The brightest of green young wheat crops are shooting up in striking contrast to the vivid red earth of the carved terraces in which the wheat and almond trees are planted.

We are driving to Ouarzazate, a primary place to pause while visiting the many surrounding kasbahs. Along the road, we pass an intermittent parade of women going to collect water, laden with huge weights of sticks or large plastic canisters on their heads. More women are set to washing clothes in the rivers, and a colourful display of laundry is spread over rocks, riverbanks and trees to dry in the burning sun. Immersed in this rural scenery, there is still a strong sense of being part of an ancient world where the rituals of life are constant.

Simple, nourishing food is what these people have eaten for centuries. Soup is an important meal in Morocco, being inexpensive and filling. Every evening during the religious month of Ramadan, it is with harira that the fast is traditionally broken.

Harira recipes vary but will most often contain some combination of dried pulses such as beans, chickpeas and lentils, fresh vegetables, mutton or chicken, and will be thickened with rice, pasta, bread or sometimes yeast. Soups will be well seasoned with pepper, chilli, saffron and other spices and more often than not will be finished off and scented with the hypnotising flavour of coriander. Harira is typically served in deep, sturdy bowls and eaten with rounded spoons carved from lemonwood – even in restaurants and street stalls you will be served harira in this way. Sweetish breads or simple flatbread, known as khubz, may be served as an accompaniment.

Here in the old medina we witness a scene that is played out every day in every Moroccan town. A child passes by ferrying a wooden board balanced on his head, topped with three flat rounds of dough neatly wrapped in a worn and faded cloth. This boy, and many other youngsters and adults like him, are on their way to the common oven. The urge to follow him is great, as is our curiosity to see inside a communal bakery.

The boy zips down the long, narrow alley and ducks into the shadow of a wide doorway. In the semi-darkness of the room, lit only by the wood-fired oven, the boy places his tray of formed bread on the floor of faded tiles, alongside other similar but different bundles waiting in turn to be baked.

The communal bakery is an ancient production line. Loaves of handcrafted bread are unwrapped and placed in the oven, in batches, in the order that they arrive. The baker tends this process, removing loaves once they turn golden brown; receiving a small amount of money for his services. When the bread is cooked, it is wrapped once again in its owner's cloth and placed on the board to be collected.

The miracle is that these masses of round flat loaves, while appearing very similar, never get confused. Once all the bread has had its time in the communal oven, how can one person's bread be recognised from another? The answer is simple. Each household will brand their loaves in some predictable way – with linear cuts, a pinch, an imprint from a fork or wooden stamp, or simply their fingertips – to differentiate their bread. Amazingly, the bakers hardly need to refer to this sign language, as after a lifetime of baking for local families they say that they can intuitively identify each individual's style of loaf. JLEC

spiced split lentil soup

IN MOROCCO, HARIRA AND OTHER NOURISHING SOUPS SUCH AS THIS ARE TRADITIONALLY SERVED IN EARTHENWARE BOWLS AND EATEN WITH UNIQUE SPOONS CARVED OUT OF LEMONWOOD.

3 tablespoons olive oil

2 onions, finely diced

2 tablespoons simple Moroccan spice blend (see page 57)

2 x 400g cans tomatoes, chopped

2 cups chicken stock (or substitute vegetable stock for a vegetarian version)

1 cup split red lentils

sea salt and freshly ground black pepper

1/4 cup chopped fresh parsley or coriander

1   Heat a large saucepan, add oil and cook onions for 3–4 minutes to soften but not colour. Add spice blend and cook for 1 minute to release essential spice flavours.

2   Add tomatoes, stock or water and red lentils and bring to the boil, then simmer for 15 minutes, stirring regularly. Add more water if the mixture becomes too thick. Season with salt and pepper to taste and serve sprinkled with chopped parsley or coriander as preferred.

SERVES 6

chickpea harira with noodles

WE WERE ABLE TO TRY MANY DIFFERENT VERSIONS OF HARIRA BY STOPPING AT THE OPEN-AIR STALLS
WITHIN THE SQUARE IN MARRAKECH. HERE, NOODLES TEND TO BE A VERY POPULAR ADDITION.

2 tablespoons olive oil

1 onion, peeled and finely diced

1 teaspoon each ground coriander and cumin

2 cloves garlic, crushed

2 carrots, peeled and diced

2 sticks celery, diced

6 cups beef stock (or substitute vegetable stock for a vegetarian version)

420g can chickpeas, rinsed and drained

100g vermicelli pasta, broken into 3cm lengths

150g green beans, trimmed and cut into 1cm lengths

1/2 cup chopped fresh parsley

sea salt and freshly ground black pepper

1   Heat a large saucepan, add oil and onion to sweat for 10 minutes over a low heat until softened but not coloured. Add spices, garlic, carrot and celery and cook for 5 minutes more, stirring regularly.

2   Add stock and drained chickpeas. Bring to the boil, then simmer gently for 30 minutes.

3   Add pasta and simmer for 5 minutes. Add green beans and parsley and simmer for a further 5 minutes. Adjust seasoning with salt and pepper to taste.

SERVES 6

bread

A strong religious sentiment surrounds Moroccan bread. In fact, all food is considered a sacred gift from Allah but bread, most especially, is important to Moroccans. Before kneading their daily bread, a cook will bless the ingredients used for making bread – the staff of life. There are many stories told of people kissing loaves of bread or gathering up a stray crust from the street and respectfully placing it somewhere safe, to honour its importance. These displays could also be interpreted as the heartfelt gestures of a community that has solemn memories of past famines.

In a land where tradition is strong, many households continue to make their own bread, usually a simple, only slightly leavened, rustic flat type of loaf. Bread is often eaten as a simple meal in itself, possibly nibbled with a few buttery textured olives. Even at elaborate feasts, bread remains an integral feature of the meal, and for special celebrations sesame seeds may be added to bread.

At every meal, flat rounds of bread are cut and laid before every person at the table. The Moroccan custom is to eat from a common dish, and so bread is used, in a way, as edible cutlery. Small pieces ripped from the loaf are held with the fingers like pincers and dipped into the sauce to scoop up pieces of meat, then the bread and meat are popped into the mouth in one delicious movement. Bread is also used to sop up the tasty juices of food, such as lusciously wet and spicy tagines; to dip into hearty soups; and to wipe the plate clean of any last drop of flavour that may have escaped and found itself there. JLEC

barley bread

IN MOROCCO, PEOPLE WHO CANNOT AFFORD WHEAT FLOUR TEND TO MAKE BREAD WITH BARLEY FLOUR. WE FOUND WE PREFERRED BARLEY BREAD AS IT HAS A MOIST CRUMB AND A WONDERFUL NUTTY FLAVOUR. TO MAKE THIS AUTHENTIC BREAD AT HOME, I BUY BARLEY FLOUR FROM MY LOCAL HEALTH-FOOD SHOP.

1/2 cup warm water

3 teaspoons active dried yeast

1 teaspoon sugar

2 1/2 cups whole wheat flour (or substitute barley flour if available)

1 cup strong flour

1 teaspoon sea salt

2 tablespoons olive oil

1 cup tepid water

extra flour for kneading

1 Place warm water in a small bowl and sprinkle with yeast and then sugar. Set aside in a warm place to activate for 5–10 minutes (when activated the mixture will be frothy).

2 Place the flours and salt in a large bowl and make a well in the centre. Pour in the frothy yeast mixture, oil and the tepid water and mix to form a firm dough. Turn dough out on a lightly floured work surface and knead for 10 minutes until smooth and elastic.

3 Divide dough in two and shape each portion into a large flat disc. Place on a lightly floured oven tray and cover with a clean cloth. Leave in a warm place to rise for 1 hour or until when dimpled with a fingerprint the dough returns to its former shape.

4 Preheat oven to 200°C. Bake for 15 minutes or until golden brown. Remove to a wire rack to cool.

MAKES 2 TRADITIONAL ROUND FLAT LOAVES

harira with chicken and green lentils

HARIRA IS A NOURISHING BROTH FORTIFIED WITH MEAT AND PULSES, AND OFTEN ACCENTED WITH THE FLAVOUR OF SPICES, FRESH CORIANDER AND THE TANG OF LEMON. TRADITIONALLY SERVED TO BREAK THE FAST DURING THE RELIGIOUS MONTH OF RAMADAN, HARIRA CAN BE A FIRST COURSE OR A MEAL IN ITSELF.

1/2 teaspoon saffron threads

1/4 cup boiling water

6 chicken drumsticks

1/4 cup olive oil

1 onion, chopped

2 cloves garlic, chopped

3 tablespoons grated root ginger

2 x 400g cans tomatoes, chopped

1/2 cup green lentils

4 cups chicken stock

1/3 cup long grain rice

juice of 1 lemon

sea salt and freshly ground black pepper

1/2 cup chopped fresh coriander

1 Combine saffron threads and 1/4 cup boiling water and leave to infuse for 5 minutes.

2 In a large saucepan, brown chicken drumsticks in a little oil for 1–2 minutes on each side, then remove to one side. Add onion and garlic to the pan, and cook over a low heat for 5 minutes to soften but not colour.

3 Add ginger, dissolved saffron, tomatoes, lentils, browned drumsticks and stock. Bring to the boil then simmer for 15 minutes. Add rice and simmer for a further 12 minutes.

4 Stir in the lemon juice and season to taste with salt and pepper. Add fresh coriander just before serving.

SERVES 6

tomato soup with couscous

THIS HARMONIOUS SOUP IS MADE MORE ROBUST BY THE ADDITION OF COUSCOUS, WHICH IS USED TO THICKEN THE TOMATO BROTH. FRESH CORIANDER IS PARTICULARLY BEWITCHING WHEN COMBINED WITH THE TANG OF TOMATOES. IF CORIANDER IS NOT A FAVOURITE TASTE, THEN I SUGGEST SUBSTITUTING PARSLEY OR MINT.

3 tablespoons olive oil

1 large red onion, finely diced

3 cloves garlic, crushed

2 x 400g cans tomatoes, chopped

2 tablespoons tomato paste

4 cups chicken stock (or vegetable stock)

1/2 cup instant couscous

sea salt and freshly ground black pepper

1/4 cup chopped fresh coriander

1 Heat a large saucepan, add oil and onion and cook over a moderate heat for 10 minutes until softened but not coloured. Add garlic, tomatoes, tomato paste and stock and bring to the boil, then simmer for 15 minutes.

2 Add couscous and simmer for a further 5–10 minutes or until couscous swells and is tender to the bite. Season with salt and pepper to taste and serve scattered with fresh coriander.

SERVES 4

todra gorge

CAEE
RESTAURANT
RENDEZ-VOUS des AMIS

THE ROAD FROM TINERHIR to the Todra Gorge meanders high above the oasis nestling along the serpentine banks of the Wadi Todra and clings to the steep sides of the eroded river gorge. Lego-like, rammed earth houses face the sun.

Below, the oasis is a vast, green sea of date palms, under which irrigation channels trickle water into the planting beds of grains and vegetables, where it is contained by low, round-topped earth walls. The flanks of these elongated mounds serve as well-trodden lanes, along which children scamper and donkeys totter. For the weak of heart but sound of rump, camels are regularly stationed by their adorned Bedouin masters to ease the steep descent down the narrow tracks to the valley floor – and then up again. An hour or two in the oasis will help erase the effects of the shambles of the nearest town to the Todra Gorge, Tinerhir. The riches created from the mining of silver in the area have sadly been spent on everything other than the pursuit of aesthetic purity.

Just up the road from the end of the oasis, the palms are replaced by boulders and the cliffs go up rather than down. Here the Wadi Todra has split open a gorge of truly daunting proportions. The pièce de résistance of this great geological fault is the cathedral-like portal where the towering cliff faces almost meet. Coming at a bend in the river, it is best viewed on foot in the still of the mid-morning. Signs warn visitors of flash floods and to steer clear of the river bank. This advice is observed by the locals but so often ignored by the drivers of camper vans looking for the perfect overnight camping spot.

Hugging the sheer rock walls, the road continues to climb up the valley to the village of Tamtattouchte. Only recently has the four-wheel drive track been replaced by a smooth, two-lane sealed road. The villagers here are gentle and blissfully naïve as to the ways of tourists. The valley floor is awash with grain and vegetable crops, plentifully irrigated by the Wadi Todra river that flows crystal clear, all year round.

On a broad ridge above the river is the densely packed village. Constructed literally from the debris of the towering mountains that surround the valley, the houses seem at one in both colour and context in this rugged mountain terrain.

Further south, the Valley du Dadès is 1500 metres above sea level and located at the foothills of the High Atlas mountain range. The road down is full of twists and turns and what appears to be one continuous village. For thirty kilometres the villages of the valley, each buoyed by the wealth generated from the fertile soil and reliable water supply, have expanded to now join as one.

Better known as the Valley of the Roses, the Valley du Dadès transforms into a profusion of colour in February. Pink and white almond blossoms precede a further colour change with the blooming of the small pink Persian roses that occupy every spare inch of the valley not dedicated to arable crops.

For Moroccans, the rose is a flower from which they produce rose water, use as a hedgerow, and value not for its beauty but for its petals. Each year, four thousand tons of petals are harvested, to be distilled locally into either rose water or exported to the perfume houses of the world. The picking of the petals is a meticulous activity undertaken by women in the cool of early morning. It is little wonder then that at the end of the season the valley is preoccupied with the event that signals the end of the harvest – the Rose Festival.

Further south again, Skoura is unlike all other palmeries – here land seems to be abundant. Scattered throughout the date palms, decaying kasbahs lie in the shadow of their restored replacements. The architectural nightmare of concrete block, now used to build family homes, has not been allowed to interfere with the regal beauty of the kasbahs. Largely uninhabited, they hint at a time when man and beast alone worked the land. A single, recently constructed, stone-covered road meanders through the outskirts of this living museum. Thankfully, this is the only apparent concession to the twenty-first century.

Crumbling gracefully, the kasbahs of Skoura sprawl enchantingly throughout the oasis. The imperfections of medieval construction methods add to the joy of beholding them. Created from the very ground on which they stand, the gently inclined, three-storey-high walls stand taupe and resolute. Crowning the four corners are sturdy towers, garlanded by crenulated parapets. As the sun dips, the bland edifice of featureless mud eases from taupe to orange, highlighting the detailed patterning, before glowing to red. JB

THE LUSH VALLEY DU DADÈS is filled with rose bushes grown for their harvest of bright pink petals, which are dried or used for the production of rose water and rose oil. Even in the off season while driving through this region it is possible to breathe in a heady rose fragrance, as this prevailing scent wafts from the rows of shops selling rose products. We stop in the town of Boumaine du Dadès, where another perfume mixes with that of roses.

Welcoming rows of conical terracotta-pottery cooking vessels sit on individual charcoal burners at a roadside café and emit a tantalising smell. These are tagines – the name that refers to both the specialised round dish of glazed earthenware with a peaked lid that fits the dish exactly, and to the recipe and the finished meal.

Each pointed tagine lid is topped with a vividly ripe tomato, positioned like a line of shiny red beacons. I'm still not quite sure why tomatoes are used in this way, as no one could directly explain this phenomenon. I wonder, perhaps when the tomato is cooked then this indicates that the tagine has also completed its cooking time? Maybe the tomato is like a plug that holds the steam inside the conical lid so that this build-up of heat gently cooks the food yet keeps it moist? Or maybe the tomatoes are a form of advertising, as they certainly attract attention! Whatever the purpose, this sight proves irresistible to our small group of hungry travellers.

We all order the special tagine of the day, which is a simple chicken stew topped with robust vegetables, scented with coriander. Each individual tomato-topped tagine is removed from the line-up and presented to us at the table. We eat directly from the cooking vessel and sop up the flavoursome juices with fragments of flatbread.

Of all the memorable tagines I have eaten throughout Morocco, the classic chicken tagine with olives and preserved lemons remains my favourite combination. There is something wonderful about the interplay of sweet chicken, salty olives and the mellow tang of lemon that appeals to my senses.

The secret to cooking a perfect tagine where the meat is divinely tender, is to simmer it slowly for many hours. Precision of timing is not important – the tagine will come to no harm if its cooking is prolonged. In fact, the flavour will be enhanced as the ingredients melt to a velvety texture.

I am reminded of one defining point of interest regarding tagines. The cooks of Fez use a different method for cooking tagines to the rest of Morocco in that they prefer not to fry their meat first, and they simply add water and rely on the ingredients to mingle and form a flavoursome stock. This refinement results in very delicately flavoured, pale, mellow tagines compared to deeper, darker versions where the meat is browned first to caramelise its natural sugars.

I recommend buying a pottery tagine in Morocco because these are excellent cooking vessels and can be hard to find out of their homeland. And because owning a tagine will forever more evocatively recall your time in this mysterious land. The tagine cooking method produces a meltingly tender stew-like meal. However, you can substitute a lidded casserole dish, if necessary, though I feel all the theatre will be gone from the cooking and presentation of this authentic meal.

If you do buy a tagine to take home it will need to be seasoned, which means that the pottery is matured, before use. I seasoned mine by following Robert Carrier's instructions in his book *Taste of Morocco*. Carrier recommends that new tagines are gently heated and flavoured with aromatics. This process removes any earthenware flavour from the new dish and aromatically impregnates the tagine with flavour that enhances future cooking. It also gently introduces the vessel to heat so that it will withstand future use over coals, on the stovetop, or in the oven.

To season a new tagine, combine 1/4 cup olive oil, a chopped onion, a couple of chopped carrots, 2 cloves of garlic and 2 bay leaves in the base of the tagine. Fill the vessel with water, cover with the conical lid and place the tagine in an oven preheated to 140°C for 45 minutes. Remove the tagine from the oven and leave to cool to room temperature before washing thoroughly. Your tagine is now seasoned and ready to produce your first delicious Moroccan recipe at home. JLEC

tagine of beef with aubergine

THIS RECIPE IS VERY MUCH MY OWN COMBINATION OF SOME DISTINCTLY MOROCCAN INGREDIENTS. LIKE ALL TAGINES (WHICH ARE ESSENTIALLY STEWS), THE SECRET TO SUCCESS IS TO SIMMER VERY GENTLY FOR A LONG TIME UNTIL THE MEAT IS MELTINGLY TENDER AND THE LIQUID IS MUCH REDUCED AND FORMS A THICK, VELVETY SAUCE.

800g stewing or braising steak

olive oil

2 onions, peeled and diced

2 cloves garlic, peeled and chopped

1/2 cup cold water

400g can tomatoes, chopped

500g aubergine (eggplant), trimmed and cubed

2 teaspoons ground cumin, toasted

sea salt and freshly ground black pepper

1 Cut steak into 4cm pieces. Heat a large frying pan, add a little oil and brown meat over a high heat for 1–2 minutes on each side. Remove to a casserole (or tagine if you have one).

2 Add onion and garlic to the pan with a little more oil and cook over a medium heat for 5 minutes. Turn up the heat and add the water, scraping the pan to remove the sediment, and simmer for 2–3 minutes to reduce by half.

3 Add tomatoes and bring to the boil, then pour over beef. Cover pan and simmer (or bake at 180°C) for 1 1/4 hours.

4 Meanwhile, in the same frying pan, with a little more oil, cook cubed aubergine for 1–2 minutes on each side until brown, then set aside.

5 After the beef has cooked for 1 1/4 hours, add browned aubergine and ground cumin to the beef and a little extra water if necessary to moisten. Bake for 45 minutes more. Adjust seasonings with salt and pepper to taste.

SERVES 6

preserved lemons

Lemons, when preserved in salt, are subdued. The natural acidic taste of the lemon is mellowed and the texture softens to an almost jam-like tenderness. Moroccan preserved lemons are called for in many recipes. They impart a very distinctive taste to dishes, which is especially highlighted, for instance, in a traditional tagine of chicken with olives and lemon (see page 112). Finely sliced or diced, preserved lemon rind makes a tart and salty garnish for salads, stews and roasts. The pickling juice, thick with salt and syrupy as honey, can be used in place of vinegar as a tangy seasoning in salad dressings. Many recipes state that the flesh should be removed and discarded from the preserved lemon before use. However, in many of the dishes we tried throughout Morocco this was not always the case.

In Morocco, lemons are usually preserved in the spring when the juicy fruit is ripe and at its best. This is how lemons are preserved in salt: take clean lemons and cut in quarters, without cutting all the way through (leaving the base intact). Cram coarse sea or rock salt generously into the cuts of each lemon; don't be afraid of using too much salt. Now pack the reshaped lemons into an appropriately sized, sterilised jar, pressing them down well. Top with a little more salt and fill any remaining space with extra lemon juice. Seal the jar and store in a cool dark place for one month before using. Shake the jar every day for the first week.

Remove lemons as required with a fork so as not to contaminate the remaining lemons. Rinse lemons with water to remove excess saltiness before adding them to food. Refrigerate once opened. Don't be alarmed if a stringy white skin forms on top of the lemons; this is harmless and can be easily skimmed off. JLEC

tagine of kefta meatballs with tomatoes and eggs

AT FIRST I WASN'T COMPLETELY SURE ABOUT THIS IDEA, HOWEVER, THE CLEVER COMBINATION OF MEATBALLS AND EGGS COOKED IN A RICH TOMATO SAUCE QUICKLY TURNED INTO A GREAT FAVOURITE.

700g lamb or beef mince

3 cloves garlic, crushed

1 teaspoon each ground coriander and paprika

1/2 teaspoon ground allspice

1/4 cup chopped fresh coriander

sea salt and freshly ground black pepper

olive oil for frying

tomato sauce (see recipe below)

4 eggs

1 tablespoon chopped fresh marjoram or parsley

1   Combine mince, garlic, spices and fresh coriander in a bowl and knead or pound until smooth in texture. Season well with salt and pepper.

2   With damp hands, mould 24 walnut-sized portions into balls and set aside on a tray.

3   Heat oil in a large frying pan and fry meatballs until golden brown all over (this will need to be done in 2–3 batches). Place meatballs in the base of a tagine or casserole.

4   Pour tomato sauce over browned meatballs. Bring to the boil, then simmer on the stovetop or bake in an oven heated to 180°C for 20 minutes, stirring once to prevent sticking.

5   Break eggs into the sauce and continue cooking for 5 minutes until eggs are just set. Scatter with marjoram or parsley and serve immediately.

tomato sauce

400g can tomatoes, chopped

1 tablespoon tomato paste

1 tablespoon liquid honey

1/2 cup hot water

sea salt and freshly ground black pepper

1   Combine all the ingredients in a bowl, seasoning with salt and pepper to taste.

SERVES 4

tagine of beef with quince

IF QUINCES ARE IMPOSSIBLE TO PROCURE OR ARE OUT OF SEASON, I RECOMMEND SUBSTITUTING APPLES OR PEARS AND PREPARING THESE BY OMITTING THE POACHING (STEP 1). SIMPLY PAN-FRY AND ADD TO THE TAGINE FOR EQUALLY DELICIOUS RESULTS.

to prepare quince

2 cups cold water

juice of 1 lemon

1/2 cup honey

1/2 teaspoon each ground cinnamon and allspice

2 quinces

olive oil

1 Place cold water, lemon juice, honey and spices in a saucepan. Peel and quarter quinces and remove cores. Slice each quarter into 3 and quickly place slices in saucepan (the lemon juice will stop them from discolouring). Bring liquid to the boil, then turn down the heat and simmer for 1 hour.

2 Remove quince slices from the liquid to drain on paper towels. Reserve the cooking liquid for the tagine. Heat a frying pan, add a little oil and fry quince slices for 1–2 minutes on each side to brown, then place to one side.

to make tagine

olive oil

1kg beef stewing steak, cut into 5cm pieces

2 onions, peeled and finely diced

3 cloves garlic, crushed

2 tablespoons finely grated root ginger

1 cup reserved quince poaching liquid or beef stock

sea salt and freshly ground black pepper

1/4 cup chopped fresh coriander

1 Heat a large tagine or casserole, add a little oil and brown meat in batches for 1–2 minutes on each side. Remove meat to one side. Add onions, garlic and ginger to the pan and cook for 5 minutes to soften and lightly brown.

2 Return meat to the pan and pour over the reserved poaching liquid or stock. Cover the pan and bring the liquid to the boil, then turn down the heat to simmer for 1 1/2 hours, turning the meat once or twice, until beef is tender and the liquid is much reduced. The cooking can alternatively be done in an oven heated to 180°C.

3 Add quince slices and a little more water if necessary to moisten the mixture and cook for 30 minutes more. Adjust seasoning with salt and pepper to taste and serve scattered with coriander.

SERVES 6

fatima's tagine of beef with artichoke stems

THE TAGINES OF FEZ (KNOWN AS THE CULINARY CAPITAL OF MOROCCO) DIFFER FROM THE REST OF THE COUNTRY IN THAT THE MEAT IS NOT BROWNED FIRST. THIS REFINEMENT PRODUCES DELICATE, PALE TAGINES WHERE THE FLAVOURS OF THE INGREDIENTS CAN BE DISTINCTLY IDENTIFIED. ARTICHOKE STEMS ARE COMMON IN MOROCCO BUT HARD TO FIND ELSEWHERE UNLESS YOU GROW YOUR OWN. I SUGGEST SUBSTITUTING FRESH OR PRESERVED ARTICHOKES AND ONLY ADDING THESE 10 MINUTES BEFORE THE END OF COOKING. THANK YOU FATIMA FOR ANOTHER GREAT RECIPE!

1 red onion, peeled and sliced

3 cloves garlic, peeled and crushed

800g beef stewing steak, cubed

2 tablespoons chopped fresh parsley

1 teaspoon ground ginger

1/2 teaspoon turmeric

1/4 cup olive oil

1/2 lemon, peeled and sliced

11/2 cups cold water or beef stock

sea salt and freshly ground black pepper

1kg artichoke stems (from an artichoke plant, picked before it flowers)

juice of 1 lemon to acidulate the artichoke water

1   Place all the ingredients, except the artichoke stems and lemon juice, in the order listed in the base of a tagine or casserole. Season with salt and pepper.

2   Cover the pan and bring the liquid to the boil, then turn down the heat to simmer for 1 hour, until the meat is tender and the liquid is much reduced. The cooking can alternatively be be done in an oven heated to 180°C.

3   Peel the artichoke stems with a vegetable peeler. Cut into 5cm lengths and place in a bowl of cold water and the juice of 1 lemon to stop them going brown. After the beef has cooked for 1 hour, add the artichoke stems to the tagine; discard soaking liquid. Cover and cook for a further 30 minutes.

4   Adjust seasoning of sauce with salt and pepper to taste and skim any excess fat from the surface before serving.

SERVES 6

berber tagine

VEGETABLES ARE THE MAIN COMPONENT OF THIS BERBER TAGINE AND ARE USED AS AN INEXPENSIVE WAY TO ADD VOLUME TO MEAT MEALS. OTHER VEGETABLES CAN BE ADDED TO TASTE; FOR INSTANCE WE REGULARLY ATE VERSIONS CONTAINING COURGETTES OR PEAS.

700g chicken portions or lamb shoulder steaks, trimmed of skin and fat, cut into 3cm strips

sea salt and freshly ground black pepper

olive oil

1 large onion, peeled and sliced

2 cloves garlic, peeled and chopped

250g carrots, peeled and sliced

800g potatoes, peeled and thickly sliced

2 cups chicken stock

3 tablespoons olive oil

1/2 cup black olives

1/4 cup chopped fresh coriander or parsley

1   Season chicken or lamb with salt and pepper. Heat a heavy-based ovenproof casserole or tagine, add a little oil and brown chicken pieces or lamb in batches for 1–2 minutes on both sides. Remove to one side.

2   Add a little more oil and the onion to the pan and cook for 5 minutes to soften but not colour. Add garlic and cook for 1 minute. Return meat to the pan and cover with layers of carrots and potatoes, seasoning with salt and pepper between layers. Pour over stock and olive oil.

3   Cover the pan and bring the liquid to the boil, then turn down the heat to simmer for 1 1/2 hours, until the meat and vegetables are tender and the liquid is much reduced. The cooking can alternatively be done in an oven heated to 180°C.

4   Scatter with olives and coriander or parsley to serve.

SERVES 6

LAMB SHANKS

lamb shanks with ras el hanout and raisins

LAMB TAGINE WITH RAISINS IS ONE OF THE CLASSIC DISHES OF MOROCCO THAT INCORPORATES RAS EL HANOUT — THE DIVINELY WARMING AND COMPLEX SPICE BLEND THAT ROUGHLY TRANSLATED MEANS 'HEAD OF THE SHOP' OR 'SHOPKEEPER'S CHOICE'.

4 lamb shanks

2 onions, peeled and sliced

2 cloves garlic, peeled and crushed

2 tablespoons ras el hanout (see page 57)

2 cups beef stock

2 tablespoons olive oil

1/4 cup liquid honey

3/4 cup raisins

sea salt and freshly ground black pepper

1 Place the lamb shanks and other ingredients in a large tagine or casserole. Season with salt and pepper.

2 Cover the pan and bring the liquid to the boil, then turn down the heat to simmer for 3 hours, turning the lamb shanks once or twice, until lamb is tender and the liquid is much reduced. The cooking can alternatively be done in an oven heated to 180°C.

3 Adjust seasoning of sauce with salt and pepper to taste and skim any excess fat from the surface before serving.

SERVES 4

tagine of chicken with prunes and almonds

MANY MOROCCAN DISHES HAVE BEEN CAST WITH A STRONG ARAB OR PERSIAN INFLUENCE. THIS IS ONE OF THOSE DISHES. DELIGHTFULLY DECORATIVE AND ALLURINGLY AROMATIC, THIS CHICKEN STEW COMBINES ALMONDS AND PRUNES AND TYPICAL SWEET AND SOUR FLAVOURS ORIGINALLY INTRODUCED FROM ARABIA.

1.4kg free-range chicken, cut into 8 portions

2 onions, thickly sliced

2 cloves garlic, peeled and crushed

1 teaspoon each ground cinnamon and ginger

1 cup pitted prunes

1 cup green olives

1/2 cup blanched almonds

1/4 cup white wine vinegar

1 1/2 cups chicken stock

sea salt and freshly ground black pepper

1/4 cup chopped fresh parsley

1 Place chicken portions in a tagine or large casserole. Scatter over remaining ingredients in the order listed, except the parsley, and season with salt and pepper.

2 Cover the pan and bring the liquid to the boil, then turn down the heat to simmer for 1 1/2 hours, turning the chicken pieces once or twice, until the chicken tests cooked and the liquid is much reduced. The cooking can alternatively be done in an oven heated to 180°C.

3 Adjust seasoning of sauce if necessary before serving. Serve scattered with parsley.

SERVES 4

tagine of chicken with lemons and olives

WE WERE SERVED MANY DIFFERENT RENDITIONS OF THIS CLASSIC MOROCCAN TAGINE. EACH
COOK WILL EXPRESS THEIR PERSONALITY BY MAKING ALTERATIONS OR REFINEMENTS, JUST AS I
HAVE DONE WITH THIS RECIPE. THIS TAGINE IS MORE TRADITIONALLY MADE WITH GREEN OLIVES
BUT BLACK OLIVES ALSO WORK WELL. THE PRESERVED LEMONS MAY BE LEFT WHOLE OR SLICED
OR CHOPPED. SOMETIMES THE CHICKEN WAS PORTIONED; OTHER TIMES IT WAS COOKED AND
SERVED WHOLE. NO MATTER THE INTERPRETATION, ALL VERSIONS OF THIS FAVOURITE DISH WERE
HAUNTINGLY MEMORABLE.

3 onions, peeled and sliced

4 chicken legs (Marylands), cut to
separate drumsticks and thighs

2 tablespoons olive oil

1 teaspoon ground turmeric

1 teaspoon ground ginger

1½ cups chicken stock

sea salt and freshly ground black pepper

2 preserved lemons, quartered and rinsed

1 cup green or black olives

¼ cup chopped fresh coriander
or parsley, as preferred

1 Place onions in the base of a tagine or casserole. Arrange
chicken portions on the bed of onions; drizzle with olive oil
and dust with spices. Pour over stock and season with salt
and pepper.

2 Cover the pan and bring the liquid to the boil, then turn down
the heat to simmer for 1½ hours, turning the chicken pieces
once or twice, until the chicken tests cooked and the liquid is
much reduced. The cooking can alternatively be done in an
oven heated to 180°C.

3 Add the preserved lemons, olives and coriander or parsley to
the sauce and cook for 10 minutes more. Skim any excess
fat from the surface before serving.

SERVES 4

ahmed's tagine of lamb with figs and sesame seeds

AHMED HOWARD DOULAKI IS THE TALENTED RESIDENT CHEF AT THE KASBAH AGAFAY. AHMED GENEROUSLY DEMONSTRATED THE MAKING OF THIS DISH ONE AFTERNOON — WE THEN HAD THE PLEASURE OF EATING THIS LAVISHLY FLAVOURED TAGINE FOR DINNER. I CAN THOROUGHLY RECOMMEND IT! AHMED SUGGESTS THAT DRIED APRICOTS, DATES OR PRUNES CAN BE SUBSTITUTED FOR THE FIGS, IF DESIRED. LIKEWISE, CHOPPED WALNUTS OR ALMONDS CAN REPLACE THE SESAME SEEDS.

1kg lamb shoulder steaks

2 onions, chopped

4 cloves garlic, chopped

1/4 cup chopped fresh coriander

2 teaspoons simple Moroccan spice blend (see page 57)

2 teaspoons ground cinnamon

1 teaspoon each ground ginger and paprika

1/2 teaspoon saffron threads dissolved in 1/2 cup boiling water

1/4 cup olive oil

sea salt and freshly ground black pepper

1 tablespoon sesame seeds

1   Trim skin and some fat from lamb and cut into 5cm pieces. Place lamb in the base of a large tagine or casserole with onions and brown over a medium heat for 5–10 minutes.

2   Add remaining ingredients to the pan, except sesame seeds. Cover pan and bring the liquid to the boil, then turn down the heat to simmer for 1 1/2 hours, turning the lamb once or twice, until lamb is tender and the liquid is much reduced. The cooking can alternatively be done in an oven heated to 180°C.

3   Adjust seasoning of sauce with salt and pepper to taste and skim any excess fat from the surface. Spoon caramelised figs over finished tagine and sprinkle with sesame seeds to serve.

SERVES 6

caramelised fig topping

2 cups dried figs

2 cups cold water

2 tablespoons sugar

2 teaspoons cinnamon

1   While tagine is cooking, simmer figs in water until softened, then add sugar and cinnamon and continue simmering until liquid is reduced and figs are caramelised.

مراكش 60

MARRAKECH 60

lies in the centre of the vast and fertile Haouz plain. Its magnetic qualities draw countless thousands of tourists to savour the sights and feel of its relaxed and inviting alleys. It was founded in 1062 by Youssef ben Tachfine, the creator of a Moroccan empire that stretched from Algiers to Spain, in an area protected from the harsh winds of the Sahara by the High Atlas mountains. The problem of a limited water supply was solved by the digging of wells linked by underground channels called khettara, a system still used to this day throughout Morocco. This enabled not only permanent habitation for the formally nomadic Berbers, but the establishment of the lush and prolific palmeries grown from the few palm trees found on their arrival.

Major building was undertaken by Youssef ben Tachfine's son, Ali Ben Youssef, largely while Youssef was off quelling the Christians in Spain. Tachfine had commenced the building process with the construction of a kasbah along with a mosque, where the Koutoubia Mosque now stands.

It was Ali who harnessed the skills of Andalucian craftsmen in building mosques, baths, palaces, extensions to the khettaras, and in 1126–27, the first of the city walls, seven kilometres in circumference. Marrakech became a centre of learning and the home of fine textiles and leather. But all was not well: alcohol was being consumed and women had taken to walking around unveiled.

Another Berber tribe, the Almohads, rode in from the Sahara, putting to death the decadent Almoravids and proceeded to build most of the great architecture of Marrakech, including the Koutoubia Mosque and the ramparts that guard the city still. In the year 1262 Morocco came under the control of the Merinids who established Fez as the capital, thereby consigning Marrakech to 300 years of stagnation until the early sixteenth century when the Saadians dispatched the Merinid rulers and re-established Marrakech as the capital. Their abundance of wealth, derived from successful forays in search of gold across the Sahara, was put to good use in the city. Only two monuments still remain from their reign: the Badi Palace, now in ruins, and the Saadian Tombs, a palace built in lavish style to house the tombs of the Saadian princes.

The contrasts with other Moroccan cities are many and varied. The wide, orange tree-lined avenues seem calm compared to those further north; the scale of the buildings, old or new, feel more compatible with human interaction and utilisation. Dominating all is the view through the fronds of the surrounding palm plantations up to the snow-capped High Atlas mountain range to the south-east of the red-hued city. Marrakech gains its wonderful colour from the soil of the surrounding plain from which the mud-brick houses and the towering protective ramparts have been made.

At the centre of it all is the Place Djemaa el Fna, from which all Marrakech is reputed to have risen, appropriately emphasised by the dominating presence of the minarets of the Koutoubia Mosque. While it is often described as a square, it is in reality a haphazard series of adjoining rectangles that form the heart of Marrakech's entertainment, shopping and dining life.

Without doubt the highlight of any visit is to eat from the nightly erected food stalls. As the evening darkens, stalls seem ablaze under a battery of electric lights and clouds of smoke billow from the charcoal grills over which the food is cooked. Aiding in the entertainment is the constant attention of the food-stall workers, who are experts at not only luring customers onto their bench seats, but keeping them amused and well-provided for. As the sun sets with vibrant orange hues behind the Koutoubia Minarets, the square becomes awash with thousands of entranced locals and visitors.

The souks inside the walls of the medina sit mostly north of Djemaa el Fna and are without doubt the best in all Morocco, mainly because of their layout, generous width of alleys and the staggering diversity of product on offer. JB

THE GREAT IMPERIAL CITY of Marrakech possesses abundant charms. Marrakech is not a city of grand monuments but it does flaunt a vividly dramatic location. Set on a plain bordering the desert, this rose-coloured city has the majestic snowy peaks of the Atlas Mountains as a striking backdrop. Fascination also lies in the heady atmosphere hidden behind the great city walls, in Place Djemaa el Fna, the main square of the medina.

Place Djemaa el Fna is undeniably the heart of Marrakech. It's impossible not to be drawn to this pulsating space, where spellbinding happenings occur daily. During daylight hours, it is alive with colourful water-sellers, snake charmers, and veiled women selling bizarre herbal remedies or rendering henna tattoos on the hands of tourists. Added to this medieval scene each night are acrobats, musicians, belly dancers, storytellers and other entertainers enacting age-old performances, surrounded by shifting circles of enthralled onlookers.

From Djemaa el Fna, several main lanes wind into the souk, which is divided into various sub-souks, each dedicated to a specific product. Strolling through the concentrated maze of paths, I found it fascinating to observe that the sights, sounds, colours and scents of the markets alter with the changing merchandise.

Souk el Attarin dispenses culinary and medicinal spices and perfumes. Here, vendors attempt to entice would-be buyers with compelling displays of live chameleons changing colour. Or, through the power of scent, by dabbing on the wrists of passing women a little hauntingly beautiful musk, jasmine or ambergris. Incense, pot-pourri and huge drifts of tiny pink rose-buds fill woven baskets and the surrounding air with pretty fragrances, which compete with those emanating from a kaleidoscope of heady spices.

Souk des Babouches houses stalls displaying the carefully stitched wares of the slipper-makers. Souk Zrabia was a slave market until 1912 – today carpets are sold here, and second-hand clothes stalls fill this space once every week. The dye merchant's souk is ablaze with vibrantly stained fabric and sequences of wool hung out to dry. And the pounding noise of hammers shaping metal commands attention throughout the smoky blacksmith's souk.

There are ceramic specialists where earthenware tagines can be purchased. An array of leather goods fills a popular thoroughfare. Turn another mysterious corner and gleaming piles of different-coloured olives appear in the olive souk, or perhaps rows of intriguing antique stores will greet you.

In the evening, the north end of Djemaa el Fna is the place people congregate – locals and visitors alike. Here, my favourite aspect of Marrakech is captured in the unfolding theatre of food stalls that magically appear, every single night of the year. To simply watch the stalls being erected at dusk provides lively entertainment that can be viewed from the rooftop balconies of various restaurants overlooking the square. But there's much more fun to be had by joining this riot of noise, people, aromas and food, all bubbling under the glow of gas lanterns.

The numbered food stalls are arranged concentrically, with each row offering an alternative dining experience. Everything imaginable (along with a few things you might prefer not to imagine) is available. Dried fruit and nut vendors and stalls selling freshly pressed orange juice line one periphery. First, there's snails cooked in great vats of broth flavoured with exotic spices. Next, a row of stalls selling steamed sheep's heads and other parts; harira; or a fascinating set-up dispensing hot mashed potato and egg sandwiches, which prove to be very popular with local diners. Plumes of smoke rise from a line-up of charcoal grills that are browning spicy coarse-textured Merguez sausages, offal, brochettes and seafood. Couscous and tagine specialists occupy the inner circle.

Most guidebooks recommend caution when eating from street stalls. However, the fact that these kitchens and their standards of hygiene are visible to diners is reassuring. We ate here several times without a problem. In fact, we gained some of our most vivid food memories from this experience.

At the far end of the profusion of savoury food stalls lie the sweetmeat booths. Here, giant copper urns hold a special tea, called khodinjal. This is an infusion of sweet spices: cinnamon, cloves and cardamom, spiked with pepper, ginger and ginseng. Huge mounds of sweetmeats called sellou are displayed beside the tea urns. Made of toasted flour, ground with seeds and nuts and spices, sellou is bound into a paste with honey, almond oil and butter. Morsels of sellou are eaten by the spoonful with sips of tea or may be presented rolled into balls that resemble chocolate truffles. Sellou and khodinjal are powerful substances, renowned for their mystical and strength-giving properties. Like all the food available in this off-beat dining theatre, well worth trying for the experience alone. JLEC

couscous salad with chickpeas and goat's cheese

THIS MODERN COUSCOUS SALAD NEVERTHELESS INCORPORATES MANY AUTHENTIC MOROCCAN INGREDIENTS. IT IS FRAGRANT, LIGHT AND TASTY, AND THE PERFECT LUNCH DISH FOR A HOT SUMMER'S DAY.

1/4 cup olive oil

1 large onion, peeled and chopped

2 cloves garlic, crushed

1 teaspoon turmeric

1/2 teaspoon cinnamon

1 1/2 cups chicken stock (or vegetable stock for a vegetarian version)

1 1/2 cups instant couscous

420g can chickpeas, rinsed and drained

150g goat's cheese, crumbled

2 red peppers, seeds removed, roasted, skinned and sliced (see tomato and red pepper salad page 142 for method)

juice of 1 lemon

3 tablespoons each chopped fresh mint and parsley

sea salt and freshly ground black pepper

1 preserved lemon (see page 100)

1   Heat oil in a large saucepan, add onion and cook over a medium heat for 5 minutes to lightly brown. Add crushed garlic, turmeric and cinnamon, and cook for 30 seconds, then add stock and bring to the boil.

2   Stir in couscous, then remove pan from the heat, cover and leave to steam for 10 minutes to soften. Remove covering and fluff up couscous with a fork. Set couscous aside to cool.

3   Toss through remaining salad ingredients, except preserved lemon, and season well with salt and pepper to taste.

4   Remove flesh from preserved lemon and discard. Rinse the rind with cold water. Finely slice rind and scatter over finished salad to garnish.

SERVES 4

kasbah couscous with perfumed chicken and seven vegetables

THIS IS THE RECIPE DEMONSTRATED BY AHMED HOWARD DOULAKI, EXECUTIVE CHEF AT THE KASBAH AGAFAY. SEVEN IS CONSIDERED TO BE A LUCKY NUMBER — FEEL FREE TO INCLUDE DIFFERENT VEGETABLES IF DESIRED BUT MAKE SURE THEY ADD UP TO SEVEN!

couscous

2 cups couscous (not instant)
1/4 cup sunflower oil
salt and freshly ground black pepper

1 Place couscous in a flat bowl. Pour oil over couscous, then rub together with your hands to coat the grains with oil so that they stay separate. The oil also helps stop the couscous from falling through the holes in the steamer.

2 Place couscous in the steamer section of the couscousiere above the chicken mixture (opposite) to steam while the chicken cooks. After 1 hour steaming remove couscous to a bowl and pour over 1 cup boiling water and rub together between the palms of your hands until the grains have swelled and the mixture feels soft like silk.

3 Return to steam for another 30 minutes. Remove and stir through salt and pepper to season.

NOTE: IF USING INSTANT COUSCOUS, THIS ONLY TAKES 5–10 MINUTES TO SOFTEN IN AN EQUAL QUANTITY OF BOILING WATER OR STOCK (SEE METHOD PAGE 122).

perfumed chicken and seven vegetables

1.4kg free-range chicken, cut into 8 portions, rinsed and dried

1 large red onion, thickly sliced

1/4 cup sunflower oil

2 teaspoons paprika

1 teaspoon ground ginger

1 teaspoon simple Moroccan spice blend (see page 57)

1/2 teaspoon turmeric or saffron powder

sea salt and freshly ground black pepper

1/4 cup chopped fresh coriander

1/4 cup chopped fresh parsley

2 cups cold water

1 cup boiling water

6 turnips, peeled and roughly sliced

6 carrots, peeled and roughly sliced

2 green peppers, seeds removed, sliced

6 baby aubergine (eggplant), trimmed and halved (or any other seasonal vegetables)

6 courgettes, trimmed and thickly sliced

3 large tomatoes, skins removed, quartered

1 Place chicken, onion, oil, spices, salt and pepper and herbs in the base of a couscousière or in a large saucepan. Cook over a medium heat for 10 minutes to lightly brown, stirring until the onion has softened.

2 Add 2 cups water and bring to the boil, then simmer for 1 hour or until chicken is cooked. Note: the couscous (previous page) is placed in the top section of the couscousière to steam. If you don't own a couscousière, then a large double boiler is a good substitute.

3 Remove chicken to one side and keep warm. Add 1 cup boiling water and the vegetables that take the longest to cook, such as carrots and turnips (not eggplant or courgettes). Simmer for 15 minutes, then add the remaining more delicate vegetables and simmer for 15 minutes more.

4 Adjust seasoning with salt and pepper to taste. Arrange chicken on top of cooked couscous and then cover with vegetables.

SERVES 6

roast chicken with date and orange couscous stuffing

COUSCOUS MAKES A FANTASTIC STUFFING FOR CHICKEN BECAUSE IT IS BEAUTIFULLY SOFT, LIGHT
AND FRAGRANT, AND EASILY TAKES ON OTHER FLAVOURS.

3/4 cup instant couscous

2 cloves garlic, crushed

6 fresh dates, pitted and roughly chopped

1/4 cup almonds, roughly chopped

finely stripped zest and juice of 1 orange

1/2 teaspoon saffron threads

1/2 cup boiling water

2 tablespoons chopped fresh mint

1/4 cup chopped fresh parsley

sea salt and freshly ground black pepper

1.4 kg free-range chicken

2 tablespoons olive oil

1 Place couscous in a bowl with garlic, dates, almonds, orange zest and juice. Soak saffron threads in measured boiling water for 2 minutes before pouring water over couscous. Stir to combine, then cover bowl with plastic wrap and leave couscous to gently steam for 10 minutes.

2 Remove covering and fluff up couscous with a fork to separate grains. Stir in herbs and season well with salt and pepper. Set aside to cool completely.

3 Preheat oven to 190°C. Prepare chicken by rinsing and drying inside and out with paper towels. Stuff couscous mixture firmly into the cavity of the chicken and tie the legs together with ovenproof string.

4 Place chicken breast-side-up in a roasting pan. Drizzle skin with oil and season with salt and pepper. Roast for 11/2 hours or until the juices run clear when a small knife is inserted deep into the thigh meat.

5 Rest for 10 minutes before carving to serve.

SERVES 6

couscous

At one time in Morocco, couscous would have been made within each family when required; the grains patiently rolled by well-practised hands. The traditional method of making couscous is very labour intensive, yet the results could be said to be worth any amount of effort – perfumed, fluffy, tender grains that are heavenly enough to make Moroccans swoon with pleasure.

Today, packets of prepared couscous and instant pre-cooked couscous are readily available from supermarkets and delicatessens. The upside of instant couscous is its fast cooking time; the downside to this adaptation is that a certain amount of taste is forfeited. However, even Moroccan cooks will use prepared couscous for convenience. Simply follow the packet instructions, and for extra flavour enrich the finished couscous with a generous measure of extra virgin olive oil or butter and fluff up the grains with a fork.

I would like to describe the making of couscous from scratch for those who may be feeling ambitious or who are interested in taking the time to experiment. Your reward will be the opportunity to taste authentic handmade couscous. There is also much pleasure to be gained from the soothing, almost therapeutic rhythm of its preparation.

Place several cups of semolina in a large bowl, make a well in the centre and sprinkle a little water into the well. With a quick hand, swirl the semolina over the centre. Sprinkle over a little salt and a tablespoon of flour and mix continuously in a circular motion with the flats of the hands. This process will form tiny grain-like bits. With a coarse-textured sieve, sift the mixture to remove any semolina that has not formed into fine palettes (couscous), which will remain in the sieve. Repeat the process, adding a little more water and flour to bind the palettes.

First, steam the couscous in a colander over simmering water or a double boiler for half an hour. Couscous is traditionally steamed in a couscousière, which is a special type of two-tiered pot, where the meat and vegetables or stew is cooked in the bottom pot and the couscous is placed in the covered steamer above. Now spread the grains out to dry in an airy place for a day. Once dried, the couscous is ready for cooking, or it can be stored in an airtight container for future use.

Before it is cooked, handmade couscous needs to be rinsed and drained, then fluffed and separated by passing the fingers through the grains. This couscous will then take up to an hour or so of steam-cooking to soften. During steaming, the couscous will need to be removed once or twice and rubbed between oiled hands so that each smooth and scented grain is separated from the others. JLEC

couscous with roast pumpkin, raisins and almonds

THIS PLEASING COUSCOUS DISH IS WONDERFULLY VERSATILE. IT MAKES A GREAT VEGETARIAN MEAL
OR ACCOMPANIMENT TO A MAIN COURSE; I'VE EVEN SUCCESSFULLY SERVED IT COLD AS A SALAD.

1/2 large pumpkin or butternut, seeds and
skin removed

olive oil

sea salt and freshly ground black pepper

1 onion, peeled and chopped

2 cloves garlic, crushed

11/2 cups chicken or vegetable stock

11/2 cups instant couscous

1/2 cup raisins

1/2 cup toasted sliced almonds

1/3 cup chopped fresh coriander

1   Preheat oven to 200°C. Cut pumpkin into 2cm cubes and
place in an oven pan. Drizzle with a little olive oil, season with
salt and pepper and toss well. Roast for 30 minutes, tossing
once during cooking, until pumpkin is tender and golden
brown.

2   Meanwhile, heat 2–3 tablespoons olive oil in a large saucepan
and cook onion and garlic over a moderate heat for 5–10
minutes, until softened but not coloured. Add stock and bring
to the boil.

3   Stir in couscous, then remove pan from the heat, cover and
leave to steam for 10 minutes to soften. Remove covering
and fluff up couscous with a fork. Season well with salt and
pepper to taste.

4   Combine couscous with raisins, toasted almonds, coriander
and hot pumpkin and toss well to serve.

SERVES 6

kasbah agafay

BEHIND HIGH ROSE-COLOURED WALLS the sound of a courtyard fountain playing on jade and turquoise tiles melodically greets guests to Kasbah Agafay. Lying just twenty minutes' drive outside the vibrant bustle of Marrakech, Kasbah Agafay is a very stylish place to rest. Located in a stunning desert setting, this private hotel displays dramatic views in every direction over olive groves, date palms, Berber villages, and beyond to the snow-topped Atlas Mountains.

One guest remarked in the visitor's book, 'Heaven and earth meet at the Kasbah Agafay', and this is so true. The red earth used to build this eighteenth-century, mud-brick castle fort, once the home of a holy man, does meet the heavenly blue Moroccan sky. Kasbah Agafay has been beautifully restored and transformed by its present owners, and offers guests a chance to enjoy a unique and extremely elegant kasbah experience.

Sequences of internal courtyards, encircled by rooms, unfold within the walls of the kasbah. Each of the private guests' rooms is imaginatively furnished with traditional textiles, tasteful antiques and objets d'art. Guests also have the choice of staying in impressive designer tents, enclosing equally lavish air-conditioned suites. These caïdal tents flaunt four-poster beds draped with antique bed covers and built-in, sculptured, mosaic bathrooms stacked with embroidered towels.

The main living rooms of the Kasbah Agafay are deliciously cool and tranquil by day. By night the walls are bathed in star-shaped shards of light shattered by the lacy-patterned surface of hand-wrought lanterns and cut-glass light-shades. Everything here is made in Morocco, from the leather ottomans, deep blood-red sofas with inlaid fabric details, and the chic armchairs, to the many gorgeous old carpets covering the floors. Crimson, lilac and gold velvet and organza drapes, tied with antique tassels, swathe enormous arched doorways. And magnificent old doors have been transformed into tabletops.

One of the kasbah's many attractions is the purpose-built health spa offering therapeutic and beauty treatments to lift the spirits. The adjoining yoga sanctuary, draped with flowing transparent veils is appropriately calm. And to complete the line-up of luxury facilities, there is also a traditional steam room, a meditation cave for deep contemplation, and a delightfully large, mosaic-tiled, outdoor swimming pool.

Another magical aspect of the Kasbah Agafay experience is that there is no set eating space – guests are free to choose a place to dine. Meals can be served inside or out, on the ramparts, or maybe on one of the many terraces or in the courtyard gardens. We enjoyed eating alfresco on a terrace with peaceful views over olive groves; and at night, in a candlelit garden courtyard where our meal was accompanied by excellent Moroccan wines from the Meknes region.

If you can bear to leave Kasbah Agafay, various choices are available to the adventurous guest. Hot-air ballooning over the surrounding desert, a visit to a local Berber village, evening horse or camel rides by torchlight, or demonstration cooking classes can all be organised, with due notice. Naturally, a cooking demonstration was at the top of my list and for this I didn't have to leave my sanctuary.

We gather in the outdoor kitchen pavilion, central to the organic vegetable and herb garden, and spend the next few hours with resident chef, Ahmed Howard Doulaki. Ahmed cooks two classic Moroccan dishes: couscous and a lamb tagine. Through demonstration and discussion, Ahmed transfers to me his knowledge of Moroccan cuisine and the history and intricacies of these recipes, along with a few personalised culinary secrets.

Firstly, charcoal braziers are fired up and fanned until the coals have burned down to glowing embers. A terracotta tagine dish is set over the brazier. Lamb is added to the dish to brown, as this will add an intensity and rich caramel flavour to the finished meal. Ahmed talks of the special (and secret) combination of spices that he likes to blend and add to food, such as this tagine. Then he strolls off to pluck a selection of vegetables and herbs directly from the surrounding garden – these will be integrated into our couscous dish.

Ahmed anoints the couscous with olive oil then tenderly caresses each particle with his fingertips to separate the grains. Once prepared, the couscous is steamed in a couscousière, using the traditional long, slow-cooking method, which takes an hour or so. A medley of garden fresh vegetables, stewed in a fragrant broth, completes the couscous dish.

This remarkable cooking demonstration turns into an amicable all-day affair and ends with elaborate feasting, as we eat the meals we have prepared. At lunch, seated in the pretty vegetable garden rotunda, we devour scented, fluffy couscous with chicken and seven vegetables. Then later, much later, we move to the candle-lit dining room and we are served succulent lamb and fig tagine. Each dish is a complete triumph. JLEG

taroudannt

AS EVENING DRAWS NEAR, the women of Taroudannt migrate to the sheltered cool of their city's towering and crenulated ramparts. Here, they promenade and then sit in familiar huddled groups. Their demure haiks, each a swathe of flowing cotton, are seemingly imbued with the colour of the indigo-blue sky above.

This daily ritual at the foot of the ramparts is one of the most peaceful scenes in Morocco. But these sunburnt ochre walls that stretch for seven kilometres around the city have also been witness to some of the bloodiest events in the land.

Constructed by the Saadians in the sixteenth century to enclose their capital, they protected the city's commerce and trade over a brief, but gloriously prosperous, period. Such was their success at trading items like cotton, sugar and indigo for gold from the Timbucktoo region that in the space of only twenty years they moved their capital north, to Marrakech's more agreeable climate. These sturdy earth walls are all that remain of this era, due to the total elimination of its residents, along with all buildings of substance by Moulay Ismael in the seventeenth century. In one foul stroke, he replaced the entire population with Berbers from the Rif area.

Remarkably, Taroudannt remains off most tourist itineraries. This may in part explain the friendly and accommodating attitude of these Rif Berber descendants. This is exemplified in the souks at the centre of the city. Both the daily Berber spice and produce market and the more permanent and extensive Arab souk are full of genial and good-spirited shopkeepers. Around the edge of one of the squares, Place Assarag near the entrance to the Arab souk, there is a plethora of cafés in which the men while away the day. In traditional style, the seats face out to ensure that everything going past gets the appropriate attention of the tea- and coffee-drinking male patrons. In the late afternoon, opportunistic stall-holders set their products out on matting all around the square, providing additional entertainment to the café dwellers, who by this time are contentedly puffing away on their shisha pipes.

Next door to one of the cafés, a camera shop advertises the brand of film that it supports with a life-size cardboard cut-out of a bikini-clad European woman. Passing the sign in droves are the haik-clad women of Taroudannt, with barely a square inch of skin showing, all seemingly oblivious to the contradiction.

Elaborately ornate horse-drawn carriages glide the streets of Taroudannt, fulfilling the role of principal taxi service for both locals and the occasional tourist alike. Life here is soothingly relaxed, in part due to the pleasantly surprising lack of motorised traffic within the walled city. Towards sunset, the peace is sometimes spoilt by the arrival of high-sided trucks at any one of the five magnificent gates that pierce the walls. They disgorge a couple of dozen women each, who, having finished their day's work on the land, join the others on the seats and ledges beneath the ramparts.

On Thursdays and Sundays, the dirt-topped paddock outside Bab el Khemis, the north-east gate, is swamped with a deluge of fresh produce and the main ingredients of all Moroccan meals – livestock. Sheep and goats throng the road to one side of the market, unaware that standing healthily to attention will negate a long walk home. The owners, sometimes of just a single sheep or goat, regale those that show the slightest interest with the extraordinary attributes of their stock. Every part of the animal is prodded, lifted and revealed to sunlight as part of the purchase process.

At the vegetable, spice and utensil stalls, the banter is similar but briefer. Bartering, the accuracy of the ancient scales and the purveyors' lightning-fast counting are the main points of the highly animated discussions.

On the periphery of the market crush, donkeys and mules contentedly consume the trimmings of the vegetables being loaded, to just below the point of topple, on the rudimentary carts to which the animals are tethered. They remain oblivious to the expanding threat to their existence posed by the ever-burgeoning fleet of trucks which form a ring around the expansive market.

Such is the volume of fresh produce on offer that it is difficult to comprehend that a mere twenty per cent of Morocco's land is deemed arable and only two per cent is planted with permanent crops. Evidence that a good proportion of Morocco's permanent cropping is to be found within the richly fertile Souss Valley can be seen on the drive in. For what seems to be a hundred kilometres, both sides of the main road are constrained by high, rammed earth walls, over which the orange orchards of the royal family can be glimpsed stretching to the valley edge.

Workers returning home carry heaving piles of orange-tree prunings for their cooking fires. There are no roadside stalls because most of the luscious fruit is exported to the markets of Europe, much of it as juice. JB

WE ARRIVE AT AN OPEN SPACE just outside the copper-coloured ramparts that surround the town of Taroudannt. It is crowded with people, ramshackle bikes, makeshift awnings and umbrellas, and row upon row of fruits and vegetables. This is Taroudannt's Berber market, held only on Thursdays and Sundays.

Berber handicrafts, we are told, are a feature of this particular market. However, as we have arrived at the time of Aid el Kebir, the Great Feast of the Lamb, it is sheep that are the focal point of today's market, and not crafts. The livestock are assembled at the far end of the market where there is colourful noise all around, and cries of sheep and goats mingle in the dusty air with those of the stall-holders.

Beside all this commotion, many everyday items can also be found. Cones of rock sugar for sweetening mint tea and coffee are done up in white or distinctive deep-purple tissue paper, and there's loose-leaf gunpowder green tea from China as well. Piles of powdered indigo (a laundry whitening agent) and handmade soaps sit among kitchen implements and hardware. Here, too, are sacks of pulses and couscous, naturally, and spices heaped in a mélange of colour.

Women wrapped in the characteristic sky-blue haiks of this region and men in plain djellabahs move between the rows of vegetables. The produce is mounded on sacking cloth or plastic sheets placed over the bare earth, yet it remains a fairly dusty scene. There are piles of potatoes, sturdy carrots, beetroot, firm red tomatoes, aubergines, cucumbers, capsicum peppers, fat broad beans and slender pea pods, variegated coloured chillies, turnips and radishes. Parsley, mint and coriander – the dominant culinary herbs – are not sold in tiny bunches here but in enormous fragrant green sheaths.

Moroccan salads incorporate all these locally grown vegetables and herbs brought in from the countryside. In Morocco, salads are served as a side dish or as an accompaniment, for instance, to a meal of kebabs or meat tagine. An assortment of salads will often be served as a first course or as part of a mezze selection at the beginning of a meal.

Salade Marocaine features on many menus throughout the land – this is a mixed salad plate of various coloured and flavoured salads. A typical combination will include arranged salads of potato, beetroot, carrot, tomato, cucumber and capsicum peppers with spiced or herbal dressings. Another salad you may come across on menus is salade a l'huile d'olive – a simple lettuce salad adorned with unctuous local olive oil. Chickpeas and lentils also feature in salads, as well as oranges and olives.

My all-time favourite salad is quite possibly the most simple of all – Moroccan tomato and cucumber salad (see page 142). I find this classic combination incredibly refreshing to eat solo; it also works well as an accompaniment to meat dishes.

After the vibrancy of the market, we decide to visit a nearby ancient synagogue on the road to Tioute. Used as an animal stall, this fortunate disguise saved the sacred Jewish site from destruction. After our visit we are invited to share tea with the synagogue's guardian. We sip tea and chat, sitting on plump, over-stuffed cushions and rush mats laid out on the bare floor of a small but brightly painted room. The walls are painted to about shoulder height with one colour; another colour covers the top section of the wall. This novel look is common and, we are told, occurs because repainting the whole room is expensive, so only the worn nether regions are retouched.

We are completely taken by surprise when our host offers us lunch, as if our spontaneous arrival had somehow been predicted. A low table is set in the middle of the room. A young boy presents us with a ewer of water perfumed with orange blossoms with which we purify our hands. The water runs into a matching receptacle, before both it and the ewer are whisked away.

Simple barley bread is placed in front of each person, then magically an earthenware tagine is produced. The lid is lifted to expose what appears to be a type of omelette, steaming hot, fragrant with spices and anointed with a generous stream of local argan oil (see page 150). We follow the lead of our host, using torn pieces of bread and the thumb, forefinger and middle finger of our right hands to gather up fragments of omelette, which has luxuriously soaked up the aromatic, nutty-flavoured oil.

This is one of the simplest yet most strikingly memorable meals of our trip. We are pressed to stay longer by our amicable host. By means of enticement he says, 'I wish you had more time. If you could stay for dinner, I would slaughter a chicken for you.' As serving meat is an important way of showing hospitality in Morocco, our host is naturally disappointed that we cannot linger. However, we depart, already honoured by his warm generosity and this unique eating experience. JLEC

tomato and red pepper salad

A SALAD MADE WITH VEGETABLES OF THE SAME COLOUR IS VERY STRIKING. THE VIVID RED OF THESE TWO COMPLEMENTARY SALAD INGREDIENTS PROVES THIS POINT. ROASTING THE PEPPERS CAUSES THEM TO PRACTICALLY MELT SO THAT THEIR JUICES FORM A FILMY VEIL-LIKE DRESSING OVER THE TOMATOES.

1kg red peppers, halved, cored and seeds removed

olive oil

500g (6 medium-sized) ripe tomatoes

2 cloves garlic, peeled and crushed

juice of 1 lemon

4 tablespoons extra virgin olive oil

sea salt and freshly ground black pepper

1 Preheat the oven to 200°C. Place the red pepper halves in an oven pan and drizzle with a little olive oil. Roast for 30 minutes or until the skins blister and the flesh is soft. Remove to a bowl and cover with plastic wrap so that the peppers sweat; this loosens their skins. Once cool enough to handle, the skins can easily be pulled off.

2 Cut tomatoes into wedges and slice roasted peppers; place in a salad bowl.

3 Combine garlic, lemon juice and oil to form a dressing and season with salt and pepper to taste. Pour dressing over salad ingredients and toss well to serve.

SERVES 6

warm potato salad

A SELECTION OF SALADS WILL OFTEN BE SERVED AS A FIRST COURSE IN MOROCCO, AND A POTATO SALAD WILL ALWAYS BE ONE OF THE STARS ON THIS PLATE.

1kg baby potatoes, washed

2 red onions, finely diced

2 cloves garlic, crushed

pinch saffron threads, soaked in 1 tablespoon warm water

2 tablespoons white wine vinegar

1/4 cup extra virgin olive oil

2 tablespoons chopped fresh coriander or parsley

2 tablespoons chopped fresh mint

sea salt and freshly ground black pepper

1 Cook potatoes in boiling salted water until just tender. Drain well, cut in half and place in a large bowl.

2 Combine remaining ingredients to form a dressing, seasoning with salt and pepper to taste. Pour over potatoes while they are still warm, then leave to cool to room temperature to serve.

SERVES 6

beetroot salad

BEETROOT SALAD PERFUMED WITH GOOD OLIVE OIL AND ORANGE FLOWER WATER IS AN ENCHANTING COMBINATION. I FIND THAT CORIANDER OR MINT ARE PARTICULARLY COMPLEMENTARY-FLAVOURED HERBS TO USE TO ADORN THIS SALAD.

1kg small beetroot, scrubbed

juice of 1 lemon

1 teaspoon ground coriander, toasted

1 teaspoon orange flower water

1/4 cup extra virgin olive oil

sea salt and freshly ground black pepper

1/4 cup roughly chopped fresh coriander, parsley or mint

1   Cook whole beetroot in plenty of boiling salted water until tender; this may take up to 30–40 minutes depending on the size of the beetroot. Drain and set aside to cool, then peel (the skins will simply slip off). Slice beetroot into wedges and place in a salad bowl.

2   Combine remaining ingredients to form a dressing, except herbs, seasoning with salt and pepper to taste. Pour dressing over beetroot and toss well. Serve scattered with chopped fresh coriander, parsley or mint.

SERVES 6

minted carrot salad

TOSSING THE CARROTS IN THE DRESSING WHILE STILL WARM WILL ALLOW THE TASTES TO INTERMINGLE AND PRODUCE A RICHER AND MORE EXCITINGLY FLAVOURED SALAD.

6 medium carrots, peeled

1 teaspoon toasted ground cumin

pinch chilli powder

2 teaspoons liquid honey

1 tablespoon white wine vinegar

4 tablespoons extra virgin olive oil

sea salt and freshly ground black pepper

3 tablespoons chopped fresh mint

1   Cut carrots into long thick strips (or rounds if preferred). Cook in boiling salted water for 3–5 minutes, then drain well and place in a bowl.

2   Combine remaining ingredients to form a dressing, except mint (so that it does not discolour), seasoning with salt and pepper to taste. Pour over carrots and toss well. Cover and set aside to cool.

3   Once cold, toss with fresh mint to serve.

SERVES 4

tuna salad with chermoula dressing

THIS COULD BE LABELLED A MOROCCAN VERSION OF THE FRENCH NIÇOISE SALAD. YOU WILL FIND
THAT THE CHERMOULA DRESSING IS A STARTLING INNOVATION.

3 cups mixed baby salad leaves

150g green beans, trimmed and blanched

370g canned tuna, drained

4 hard-boiled eggs, shelled and quartered

4 small tomatoes, quartered

sea salt and freshly ground black pepper

1 cup chermoula (see page 71)

lemon wedges to garnish

1   Place a bed of lettuce leaves in a large bowl. Arrange beans, tuna, quartered eggs and tomatoes on top of lettuce. Season with salt and pepper.

2   Drizzle salad with chermoula to dress and serve with lemon wedges to garnish.

SERVES 4

moroccan tomato and cucumber salad

THIS SALAD IS SIMPLICITY ITSELF AND THE MOST DELICIOUSLY PALATE-COOLING COMBINATION TO
ENJOY ON A HOT MOROCCAN DAY. IT MAY BE EATEN AS A REFRESHING STARTER OR IT CAN FORM A
SALSA-LIKE ACCOMPANIMENT THAT IS OFTEN SERVED BESIDE GRILLED MEAT BROCHETTES.

5 medium-sized ripe tomatoes, seeds removed

1 telegraph cucumber, seeds removed

1 red onion, peeled

1 green pepper, core and seeds removed

1/2 cup chopped fresh parsley

1 teaspoon ground cumin, toasted

juice of 2 lemons

3 tablespoons extra virgin olive oil

sea salt and freshly ground black pepper

1   Finely dice the tomatoes, cucumber, onion and green pepper and place in a large bowl.

2   Combine with remaining ingredients, seasoning well with salt and pepper to taste.

SERVES 4–6

chickpea and spinach salad

IT IS VERY WORTHWHILE TO TAKE THE TIME REQUIRED FOR SOAKING AND COOKING DRIED
CHICKPEAS. THE DIFFERENCE IN FLAVOUR AND TEXTURE IS INCOMPARABLE.

1½ cups dried chickpeas
1 green pepper, seeds removed, finely diced
2 cups baby spinach leaves
4 cloves garlic, crushed
2 teaspoons wholegrain mustard
finely stripped zest and juice of 1 lemon
¼ cup extra virgin olive oil
sea salt and freshly ground black pepper

1   Soak chickpeas overnight in plenty of cold water.

2   Next day, drain chickpeas, place in a saucepan and cover
    with fresh cold water. Bring to the boil, then simmer for 1 hour
    or until chickpeas are very tender. Drain well and set aside to
    cool.

3   Combine cold chickpeas with remaining salad ingredients
    in a bowl. Combine remaining ingredients to form a dressing,
    seasoning with salt and pepper to taste. Pour over salad and
    toss well to serve.

SERVES 6

argan oil

The argan tree is extraordinary. Native to North Africa, it has spiky branches that goats have an inclination to climb and graze. The large, vivid green, olive-shaped argan berries are harvested in May and June. They are left to dry for several months, then cracked open with a rock to release their seeds. The seeds are toasted in a large flat pan over an open fire and swirled around by hand so that they do not catch and burn.

In a laborious hands-on process, the toasted seeds are ground between two specially hewn granite stones. A thick burnt-toffee brown paste is formed, and it is impossible to imagine how this can be separated to release the essential oil. Slowly and deliberately, water is added to the mix and in a surprising display of alchemy the mixture begins to separate. Aicha, our guide to this remarkable process, assists this division by expertly squeezing together clumps of the now malleable Plastercene-like paste so that a trickle of pure argan oil seeps out between her fingers. It takes the fruit from thirty argan trees and three hours' hard labour to produce one litre of this pure oil.

It is impossible to describe the taste of argan oil, as there really is nothing quite like it. It has a nuttiness that comes from the toasting process and is appealingly unctuous, being thicker and more viscous than olive oil. It has to be said that it has a distinctive taste of argan oil! However, as it is not readily available outside Morocco, it would be possible to substitute toasted almond or walnut oil, as these have a closely related toasted nutty flavour, or a flavoursome extra virgin olive oil in recipes.

Argan oil is traditionally sold by the side of the road. A special ground paste of almonds and argan oil bound with honey or sugar, called amlou, can also be purchased from roadside vendors. This mixture is eaten on bread for breakfast or as a snack. Pure argan oil can be used to anoint foods, such as omelettes (see page 23), vegetables or tagines, or mixed in salad dressings in place of olive oil. JLeC

essaouira

ESSAOUIRA MIGHT NOT BE EASY TO SPELL, but it's easy to like. After the colourful crush of Marrakech or tourist-orientated Agadir, Essaouira appears calm, clean, relaxed and orderly. A favourite haunt in the 1970s of musicians Cat Stevens and Jimmi Hendrix, Essaouira still seems to have a profound effect on visitors today. It is a coastal town, full of integrity, relying on doing two things well: fishing and looking after a small but growing number of tourists.

There is no need to arrive in Essaouira with a fixed agenda or a sense of urgency to see the sights. Special places, while few, remain largely unchanged since 1760 when Mohammed II commissioned the French architect Theodore Cornut to build a naval base.

Today the influences of Africa, Europe and Arabia can still be glimpsed among Cornut's port and his European-styled fortresses surrounding the medina.

A massive seawall shelters the port from the heaving swells of the Atlantic and provides the perfect platform for fishing duties. Nets are mended, hooks are baited and boats moored, maintained and repaired using time-proven methods. Gulls wheel overhead as the night's catch is manhandled ashore from reggae-coloured trawlers. The gathering crowd, ever keen to barter for the choicest, still-flapping fish, vie for gangplank's end, coins and crumpled notes at the ready.

Nestled behind the trawlers are moored hundreds of five-metre long, baby-blue sardine boats, packed jigsaw-tight against each other. Although these may appear to be the poorer cousins of the bigger trawlers, their stout-framed hulls and centuries-old design have ensured that Essaouira's history of sardine fishing continues. Towards sunset, at the mouth of the harbour, an ant-like flotilla of these boats can be seen heading west. Hardy fishermen sit aboard their craft with a casualness born through generations of association, while their women, swathed in haiks, resemble sitting pears as they gather under the city's ramparts, pondering the day's events.

Inside the ramparts, Essaouira's well-preserved medina boasts a meeting place little altered over three hundred years. This preservation has been aided of late by the city fathers' enlightened policy of restricting the outward expansion of the town. Hence, some ten kilometres shy of town, hundreds of new apartments are being built, and within the medina itself major reconstruction of the Mellah area, the Jewish Quarter, is underway. It is hard to comprehend when visiting Essaouira today that the town declined so dramatically after the Jewish community departed following the French establishing Casablanca as the commercial centre of Morocco.

If relaxing and doing next to nothing leaves you wanting more, then only a little more is what you'll find just outside Essaouira. Thirty kilometres south is Sidi Kaouki, now mainly frequented by windsurfers who put to good use the area's constant trade winds. It is also where you'll find the marabout of Sidi Kaouki after whom the town is named. Crumbling and perched on a rocky jut at the northern end of the beach, this sacred tomb, once believed to cure infertility, now stands abandoned but for the occasional tourist.

It was on the day we went to Sidi Kaouki that we discovered the correlation between the argan trees studding the bleached, taupe, coastal hills and the simple roadside stalls selling amber liquid in a variety of recycled plastic bottles. On first inspection it looked suspiciously like engine oil but was in fact argan oil, a product only produced in Morocco, and while possessing qualities of olive oil is actually sweeter and richer in taste.

One of the roadside traders, Azaroual Houssein, not content with merely showing us the product, insisted on taking us to his house to view the method of manufacture. Aicha, his sister-in-law, though somewhat surprised at having an audience, graciously set about a two-hour production exhibition with remarkable agility and poise. JB

THE ATLANTIC PORT OF ESSAOUIRA is a great place to try Moroccan specialty fish dishes. Such a meal may take the form of a simple plate of fried sardines consumed at an open-air café or a complex-flavoured fish tagine in one of the restaurants within the town's fortified walls.

Today Moroccan cuisine is relatively unified, however there are some subtle variances that can be noted. These differences are mostly linked to produce at hand, and climatic or regional idiosyncrasies. Naturally, specialty seafood dishes are associated with the coast where the sea still freshly delivers catches of fish. There are some other distinctive aspects, for instance, a strong Jewish community in Essaouira has contributed to the presence of Jewish-influenced specialty dishes, such as fish balls (see page 165).

Throughout Morocco, chermoula is the most common marinade for fish (see page 71). However, on the coast tomatoes are more frequently included in fish tagines than in those made in the interior regions. Sometimes whole fish will be stuffed with a delectable, rich tomato jam known as matecha m'assala in Moroccan or by its French name, confit de tomates. This preparation is basically a spiced tomato sauce that is so well reduced that it becomes thick and sticky, like jam (see page 72).

On our first morning's exploration of Essaouira we buy paper cones filled with chickpeas liberally dusted with cumin salt. We nibble this simple snack food and walk along the manicured beach, adorned in the European fashion with deck-chairs and straw umbrellas. When we arrive at the port we watch the colourful activity provided by fishing boats unloading their various catches. There are cases of sardines that have already been salted at sea; large blue crabs with bound claws; and a wide assortment of fish, many of which will soon appear on the menus of the local eateries.

As we meander beside the sea-wall towards the town, we discover a cluster of outdoor grill cafés under a row of blue-and-white striped canvas awnings. This is where we enjoy one of the best fresh fish meals in Essaouira. There is a procedure to obey. Diners first choose their preferred fish from concrete slabs displaying the day's catch. Your chosen fish is then cleaned, opened out like a butterfly, sandwiched between a wire cage and barbecued over charcoal embers, while you wait, seated on one of the narrow wooden benches, in mouth-watering anticipation.

Eating a plate of fried sardines is one of the truly authentic taste experiences available. We found the best approach for consuming a huge plate of small fish is to follow the etiquette of local diners. They nimbly pick and nibble the delicious flesh from the bones, discarding the bones onto the tabletop. At the end of the meal the paper tablecloth will be embroidered with neat piles of feathery fish bones. This makes for an easy clean-up, as the whole lot can be bundled up and disposed of to be replaced with a clean paper cloth.

Morocco's Atlantic coast is varied and fascinating. One day we drive north from Essaouira to investigate the primordial-looking salt flats at Oualidia. Here, in an estuary at the top of a lagoon, huge mountains of raw salt form an eerie sight. Salt is a vital substance used to preserve many important Moroccan food products. Olives are cured in salt, sardines are salted, and lemons and pickled vegetables are preserved in copious amounts of salt.

On our original drive into Essaouira from Taroudannt, via Agadir, we passed through the small town of Tamri. A colourful sign advised us that the local banana souk was in full swing. Sunny yellow canvas booths lined the road; each displaying nothing but bunch after bunch of bananas, which we later saw growing in the surrounding sub-tropical river basin.

Close to Essaouira, we pass rolling fields of native argan trees, with their distinctive spiky branches and bright green berries. At roadside stalls, patient men squat or stand in pointy hooded djellabahs watching over precious bottles of hand-pressed argan oil (see page 150). They also sell amelou, a paste of ground almonds, honey and argan oil that is spread on bread and eaten as a snack or for breakfast.

In this part of the land, many small whitewashed villages quietly reside under a perfect blue sky. The red soil is awash with small purple-blue flowers, and the terrain could be compared to the rugged coasts of Spain or Greece. Everything is blue or white. Houses, shops and women's haiks are white; and tiles, distinctive inlaid metal doors, and even the petit taxis here are blue – it's as if the azure sky has fallen down to earth in patches. JLEC

prawn pil pil

PRAWN PIL PIL APPEARS ON MANY MENUS, ESPECIALLY IN TAROUDANNT, ESSAOUIRA AND ALONG THE ATLANTIC COAST. BEWARE, THOUGH, AS SOME VERSIONS ARE MUCH HOTTER THAN OTHERS.

3 tablespoons olive oil

2 onions, peeled and diced

2 cloves garlic, peeled and crushed

1 teaspoon each paprika and chilli flakes

2 x 400g cans tomatoes, chopped

sea salt and freshly ground black pepper

700g prawns, heads and shells removed, leaving tails intact

3 tablespoons chopped fresh parsley

1　Heat a large saucepan, add oil, onions and garlic and cook for 10 minutes over a gentle heat until softened but not coloured. Add paprika and chilli and cook for 1 minute.

2　Add tomatoes and bring to the boil, then simmer for 10 minutes to reduce liquid and thicken. Season with salt and pepper to taste.

3　Remove and discard the dark vein running down the backs of the prawns. Add prawns to the pan and simmer for 5 minutes until prawns have turned pink and are cooked. Serve scattered with parsley.

SERVES 4

baked sardines with tomatoes

WE SAW MANY TEMPTING TRAYS OF THESE SARDINES BEING PARADED THROUGH THE SOUKS ON THEIR WAY TO THE COMMUNAL BAKERY OVENS WHERE THEY ARE COOKED UNTIL GOLDEN BROWN.

1kg fresh sardines, gutted and cleaned

6 ripe tomatoes

olive oil

freshly ground black pepper

1　Preheat oven to 180°C. Arrange sardines in a single layer in a large oven pan. Place tomatoes on top. Drizzle with olive oil and season with pepper.

2　Bake for 30 minutes until sardines are golden brown and tomatoes bursting with juice.

SERVES 6

sardines

Great oven trays of fresh sardines, adorned with tomatoes and peppers and besprinkled with olive oil are marched through the narrow lanes of the medina on their way to the communal bakery. When a space is available among the loaves of bread, the sardines take their turn in the wood-fired oven. These pungent little fish emerge roasted to golden brown and the tomatoes have melted to moisten their rustic, salty flesh. This treatment of sardines epitomises the honesty of Moroccan home cooking.

Cafés along the coast from Safi to El Jadida specialise in locally caught sardines. More often than not, they are served simply grilled or fried, and unadorned to emphasise their natural taste. Diners tuck in to plates of whole fish with relish, picking at the briny flesh with their hands and discarding the bones. At the end of the meal, entwined stacks of discarded fish bones ornament the paper-clad tabletop, like delicate and frivolous sculptures. JLEC

saffron fish tagine with pine nuts and raisins

ONCE AGAIN THE INFLUENCE OF ARABIA IS EVIDENT IN THIS SWEETLY SAVOURY FISH DISH THAT IS
OPULENTLY DECORATED WITH PINE NUTS AND RAISINS.

2 tablespoons olive oil

3 onions, finely sliced

1/2 teaspoon saffron threads soaked in
1/4 cup boiling water

1/4 cup white wine vinegar

2 tablespoons raisins

3 tablespoons toasted pine nuts

800g white-fleshed fish fillets, such as
cod or snapper

sea salt and freshly ground black pepper

olive oil for frying

3 tablespoons chopped fresh coriander

1 Heat a frying pan, add oil and onions and cook over a
   moderate heat for 10 minutes until softened and slightly
   caramelised. Add saffron and soaking liquid, vinegar, raisins
   and pine nuts, then simmer for a further 2–3 minutes.

2 Season fish with salt and pepper. Heat the base of a tagine
   or non-stick frying pan, add a little olive oil and pan-fry fish until
   golden brown on both sides. Spoon onion mixture over fish,
   cover pan and simmer for 4–6 minutes to finish cooking fish.
   Scatter with coriander to serve.

SERVES 4

tagine of fish balls

I ATE A VERSION OF THIS FASCINATING FISH-BALL TAGINE IN A RESTAURANT OF THE HYATT IN CASABLANCA. THIS IS MY INTERPRETATION OF THAT MEMORABLE DISH.

1kg boneless white-fleshed fish, such as snapper or cod, roughly cubed

1/2 cup fresh breadcrumbs

3 cloves garlic, crushed

1 small red chilli, seeds removed and finely chopped

3cm piece root ginger, finely grated

1/2 cup chopped fresh coriander

1 egg white, lightly beaten

juice of 1 lemon

sea salt and freshly ground black pepper

olive oil for frying

2 onions, finely diced

1 teaspoon ground ginger

1/2 teaspoon saffron threads, dissolved in 1/4 cup boiling water

1 preserved lemon, pulp removed and discarded, rind diced

1 cup fish stock

3 tablespoons chopped fresh parsley

1   Place cubed fish in the bowl of a food processor and process to form a rough-textured paste. Transfer to a bowl and combine with breadcrumbs, garlic, chilli, root ginger, coriander, egg white and lemon juice. Season with salt and pepper and mix well. Shape with damp hands into 24 walnut-sized balls.

2   Heat a frying pan, add a little oil and gently fry fish balls in batches until browned all over. Remove to one side.

3   In the same pan add a little more oil and sweat onions for 5 minutes until softened but not coloured. Add ground ginger, saffron and soaking liquid, diced preserved lemon rind and stock. Bring to the boil, then simmer for 10 minutes.

4   Return fish balls to the pan, cover and cook gently for 10 minutes. Scatter with parsley to serve.

SERVES 4

chermoula fish tagine

CHERMOULA IS A CLASSIC MARINADE FOR FISH. I FIND THAT THE SPICES INCLUDED IN THE CHERMOULA MIX LEND A PENETRATING, ALMOST CURRY-LIKE FLAVOUR TO THIS TAGINE.

4 large carrots, peeled and thickly sliced on the diagonal

4 sticks celery, thickly sliced on the diagonal

1/2 cup water

sea salt and freshly ground black pepper

4 tomatoes, thickly sliced

800g white-fleshed fish fillets, skin and bones removed

1 cup chermoula (see page 71)

fresh or preserved lemon wedges to garnish

1 Place carrots and celery in the base of a large tagine or casserole. Add 1/2 cup water and season with salt and pepper. Arrange tomatoes on top and then fish. Pour chermoula over fish.

2 Cover pan with lid, place over a gentle heat and cook for 30–40 minutes or until fish is cooked and vegetables are tender.

3 Serve with lemon wedges.

SERVES 4

architecture

Morocco reveals at every turn a very distinctive Arab style. The cultures of Portugal, Spain, France, and the nations of the Middle East have all left their unique influence. However, the colour and texture of what has developed over the centuries is now universally recognised as Moroccan. JB

the atlantic coast

TERRACOTTA, BLOOD RED, washed-out lemon and a multitude of blues – in any other context the mix would be incongruous. But under a brilliant blue sky, in the unhurried, cobbled walking lanes of Azemmour's medina, the colour fusion is at once perfect.

The small city of **Azemmour** perches high above the Atlantic coast and a wide and languid river, Wadi Oum er-Riba. It is from these two waterways that its architectural influence has evolved. Wadi Oum er-Riba's source is in the very heart of Morocco, borne from the snows of the High Atlas. The grains that have been grown for centuries on the river's well-irrigated banks were the trading catalyst for regular visits by the Carthaginians, Romans and Portuguese. The Portuguese were so enamoured with Azemmour that they repeatedly tried to make it their own, finally succeeding in 1513. Their brief occupation saw the construction of the kasbah, watch towers, and the ramparts that provide the perfect platform on which to take an aerial tour of the city. At street level, the doors of houses flanking the narrow lanes are spectacular. What they lack in height, they more than make up for with their vivid colour, heavy metal studding and impenetrable sturdiness. Fatima's protective hand appears in some form on every door. The wonder of the spic and span Azemmour is that it is almost completely untroubled by the pace of modern life, traffic or tourists.

El Jadida, once known as Mazagan, was a major, well-fortified trading port until the Portuguese were driven out by Sultan Sidi Mohammed in 1769. The Portuguese act of dynamiting and burning the city on their hurried departure determined the rebuilding of the city and the renaming of it as El Jadida (New City).

The Old Portuguese quarter, still staunchly enclosed within towering ramparts, is without doubt one of the highlights of Morocco – if only for the walk atop the ramparts. From the south-eastern tower in the late afternoon, a cavalcade of small wooden fishing boats can be observed, chugging back into port. Within the walls, life is low-key. While the real shopping action is happening in the market souks outside the walls, the small, single product shops inside that sell everything from bread to charcoal reveal the simple daily needs of the town's inhabitants.

A sixteenth-century underground cistern in the centre of the old quarter began its life as a magazine and was then converted into a reservoir. With the demise of the old quarter in the mid-1800s, the cistern was forgotten and only rediscovered in 1916. Reflections from the Gothic-styled, stone-arcaded roof can be seen in the still waters beneath.

The majority of the residents of **Safi** rely for their living on the city's sardine and phosphate processing plants. The plethora of sardine processing and canning plants dominating Safi's southern end, is just a hint at the scale of the sardine-fishing industry. Morocco is the largest processor and exporter of sardines in the world. Each year, in excess of 400,000 tons of migrating sardines is netted by a fleet of some 500 twenty-metre wooden trawlers plying the shoals off the Atlantic coast. Safi is perfectly located at the centre of these major sardine-fishing grounds.

Outside the ramparts, to the immediate north of the town, is the Colline des Potiers. Drying pottery, raw and regimented on every available level surface, decorates the hillside on which low-slung buildings and the beehive-shaped kilns of the Colline des Potiers are haphazardly crammed. The kilns, some hundreds of years old, are progressively stacked to bursting point before being bricked in and wood-fired. Within buildings alongside the kilns, potters sit on the edge of holes in the bare earth floor. They guide mounds of moist, gently spinning clay into shapes that are the exact replica of all previous throws. The wheels are powered by the potter's bare feet, rhythmically propelling a large, flat-worn, round-edged stone. Higher up the hill, colour is deftly applied to all manner of ceramics by brushes held in the assured hands of craftsmen hunched over their work. The only illumination for this intricate work is often one thin shaft of light coming from a rent in the earthen wall.

The coastal road between Safi and Azemmour, and then up to the outskirts of Casablanca, is a fitting conclusion to any journey. Alongside the road, a broad swathe of sand is shaped by the gentle swells of the Atlantic. Fishing villages nestle beside estuaries and natural harbours protected by rocky outcrops. Stout wooden fishing boats are manoeuvred only with oars the size of small telegraph poles. They wait to time their run to shore on the crest of waves surging through the narrow channel. Waiting for them on shore are a dozen men, ready to haul the craft beyond the high-water mark before partaking of the ritual inspection and purchase of the day's catch. JB

MOROCCAN SWEETS AND PASTRIES are intoxicating combinations, bound with delicate perfumes, sticky syrups, heavenly tastes and lyrical names. Cigar-shaped pastries with a nutty sweetmeat filling go by the name of Fatima's fingers. The serpent cake is a large snake-like coil of sweetly stuffed pastry containing dates, figs or nuts, liberally dusted with icing (confectioner's) sugar. There is a great tradition of numerous honeyed cakes, rich pastries for feast days and a wide range of simple biscuits.

The Moroccan's love of pastry takes many hypnotic forms. The possibilities are seemingly infinite: from sheets and ribbons to rolls, triangular parcels and envelopes. Baked or fried, some pastries are bathed in rivulets of thick, perfumed syrup while others encase fillings of cream, dried fruits or pulverised nuts. And all these spellbinding delights are habitually enjoyed with tiny steaming glasses of sweet Moroccan mint tea.

Perhaps the most famous Moroccan pastry of all is the crescent-shaped ka'b ghzal, so called because each pastry-wrapped sweetmeat is delicately shaped to represent the curve of a gazelle's horn. However, our friend Fatima told us, on good authority, that the true translation and shape typifies a gazelle's slim ankle, not the horns. These pretty pastries are either served plain or they may be dipped in orange flower water, then rolled in a thick coating of icing sugar.

Fatima demonstrates the making of ka'b ghzal, which requires great dexterity, skill and, I imagine, years of practice. The filling is a sweet almond paste, bound with the perfumed addition of orange flower water, which Fatima distils herself from each year's crop of orange blossoms. The special pastry is rolled extraordinarily thin and cut to enclose elongated portions of filling, then each is shaped to resemble the slender ankle of a gazelle. Once cooked, the pastry casings are pale and crisp and the filling turns delightfully chewy. We devour several immediately – eaten freshly made, gazelle's ankles are completely irresistible and extremely moreish.

The Moroccan's great affection for sweetness is symbolised by the number and quality of sweet shops throughout the land. One such store we stopped to admire in Marrakech was like an Aladdin's cave, bursting with jewel-like pastries and lavish sweet morsels. The scent of honey, rose and orange flower waters was thick in the air. There were pyramids of dates stuffed with pink- or green-sugared almond paste, intense whirls of intricate pastries and neat piles of little biscuits. And in pride of place, a platter of perfect gazelle's ankles. In Morocco, sweet pastries like these may be served before a meal, whenever guests arrive, or simply for morning or afternoon tea.

Desserts are not traditionally served at the end of a meal, as Westerners might expect. Fresh fruit often signals the end of a daily meal. Desserts are mostly reserved for special occasions or to honour guests. And good restaurants will cater to the tastes of visitors by offering desserts in the Western tradition.

The most elaborate Moroccan dessert is considered to be sweet b'stilla, where layers of tissue paper-thin wharka pastry are cooked under a showering of ground almonds, sugar and cinnamon, and served with an almond milk sauce to moisten the crisp pastry sheets (see page 38). This complex and dizzying creation is usually served at banquets. However, travellers can taste this delight for themselves in some of the smarter restaurants in major Moroccan cities.

My favourite Moroccan sweet treats are those available on the street. I'm addicted to the chewy, sugary macaroons sold by veiled women in the souks of Marrakech. The pastel-coloured blocks of nougat, sliced and sold by weight, available from sellers who push handcarts through the market lanes, are equally addictive. Caramelised nuts or toffee-bound blocks of sesame seeds (the sesame seed shrub actually grows in Morocco) are another commonly found street-stall confection. All are guaranteed to pep up energy levels during souk shopping sprees.

In El Jadida, we meet a charming young woman working in a street-front booth making what looks like a combination of thin puff pastry and a giant pancake. This we discover is maloui, made of thinly rolled sheets of lightly leavened dough, interleaved with oil or butter and folded to create a flaky-textured pastry. Once fried to golden, portions are cut to the customer's requirements, then saturated in liquid honey and wrapped in paper for easy transportation. We join the queue of locals to buy fragments of maloui to nibble as we explore the streets of El Jadida and wander through a vibrant street souk towards the fortified sea-wall. JLEC

macaroons

VEILED WOMEN SELLING TRAYS OF HEAVENLY SWEET MACAROONS CAN BE FOUND IN MANY OF
THE SMALL ALLEYWAYS THAT MAKE UP THE GRAND SOUK IN MARRAKECH. I COULD NOT RESIST
BUYING THESE SWEET TREATS WHENEVER I PASSED A VENDOR, AND EVEN NOW THEIR TASTE AND
TEXTURE REMAIN VIVIDLY MEMORABLE.

2 large egg whites
2/3 cup caster sugar
1 teaspoon liquid honey
1½ cups ground almonds
1 tablespoon flour

1 Heat oven to 160°C on fan bake (or 175°C conventional oven) and line 2 baking trays with non-stick baking paper.

2 Place egg whites, sugar and honey in a bowl set over a pan of simmering water and whisk until mixture is very pale and sugar has dissolved (about 5 minutes). Remove from heat, then stir in almonds and flour. Leave to stand for 15 minutes.

3 Place tablespoons of the mixture on prepared baking trays, allowing space for the mixture to expand as it cooks. Bake for 15–20 minutes or until golden brown. Remove to cool on trays for 5 minutes before transferring to a wire rack to cool completely. Store in an airtight container.

MAKES 16

date tarts

DATES ARE ONE OF THE MOST ENCHANTING INGREDIENTS USED IN MOROCCAN COOKING AND THEY ARE ALLOWED TO TRULY SHINE IN THESE PRETTY LITTLE TARTLETS.

pastry

1 cup plain flour
2 tablespoons caster sugar
75g butter, melted and cooled

1 Place flour and sugar in a bowl. Stir in butter to form a crumbly dough. Press dough into 10 small tart tins. Prick bases and chill for 30 minutes.

filling

50g butter, softened
2 tablespoons caster sugar
1 small egg
1 tablespoon finely grated root ginger
1/2 cup ground almonds
2 tablespoons plain flour
10 fresh dates, pitted and halved
2–3 tablespoons liquid honey to drizzle
icing sugar to dust

1 Preheat oven to 190°C. Place butter and sugar in a bowl and beat to combine. Add egg and ginger and beat well. Stir in ground almonds and flour to form a paste. Spread a layer of paste over the base of each pastry case.

2 Arrange 2 date halves on the surface, pressing these slightly into the almond paste.

3 Bake for 15 minutes or until golden brown. Serve drizzled with honey and dusted with icing sugar.

MAKES 10

oranges with cinnamon and flower-water syrup

THIS IS ONE OF THE TYPICAL DESSERTS THAT CAN BE FOUND ON MENUS IN MOROCCO. WHILE THIS DISH IS ESSENTIALLY SIMPLE, THE COMBINATION OF FLAVOURS LIFTS ORANGES TO MAGNIFICENT HEIGHTS.

1/2 cup sugar
1/2 cup honey
1 teaspoon ground cinnamon
2 teaspoons orange flower water
1 cup cold water
4 oranges, peeled and sliced

1 Place sugar, honey, cinnamon, orange flower water and cold water in a saucepan and bring to the boil, stirring until sugar dissolves. Turn down the heat and simmer gently until reduced by half.

2 Place the orange slices in a bowl and pour over hot syrup. Set aside to cool and for flavours to infuse.

SERVES 4

ORANGES WITH CINNAMON AND FLOWER-WATER SYRUP

gazelle's ankles

KA'B GHZAL ARE ONE OF THE MOST FAMOUS SWEETS OF MOROCCO. THESE EXQUISITE, CRESCENT-SHAPED PASTRIES STUFFED WITH A CHEWY, ORANGE FLOWER WATER-SCENTED ALMOND PASTE ARE USUALLY SERVED WITH STEAMING GLASSES OF MINT TEA. THERE IS SOME CONTENTION AS TO WHETHER HORNS OR HOOVES ARE THE TRUE TRANSLATION OF KA'B GHZAL. HOWEVER, FATIMA, WHO KINDLY SHOWED ME HOW TO MAKE THESE BEGUILING TREATS, TELLS ME THAT THEY ACTUALLY REPRESENT THE SLENDER ANKLES OF THE GAZELLE.

1 cup plain flour

pinch salt

1 tablespoon melted butter

1 tablespoon sunflower oil

1 teaspoon orange flower water

1. Place flour and salt in a large mixing bowl and make a well in the centre. Place melted butter, oil, orange flower water and enough warm water to make into a firm dough. Mix by hand, then turn out onto a bench and knead for 2 minutes.

2. Roll the ball of dough around in a bowl smeared with a little oil. Cover with plastic wrap and place in the fridge for 1–5 hours. Prepare the filling.

filling

500g blanched almonds

250g sugar

1/2 teaspoon mastic powder, if available

2 teaspoons melted butter

1 teaspoon sunflower oil

1 tablespoon orange flower water

1. Preheat oven to 170°C. Grind the almonds in a food mill until very fine. Add sugar, mastic, butter, oil and orange flower water and process to combine into a solid paste.

2. Shape almond paste into long, thin, sausage shapes approximately 1/2cm x 5cm. Roll out a portion of the pastry extremely thin.

3. Place an almond sausage in the centre of the pastry; pull and stretch the pastry over the filling. Press the filling between your thumb and index finger into a high crescent shape. Cut the pastry around the filling with a fluted pasta-cutting wheel. Place on a lightly oiled baking tray and prick 3–4 times with a needle to release air during cooking. Repeat the process with remaining ingredients.

4. Bake for 15–20 minutes or until golden brown. Gazelle's ankles will last for 1 month in an airtight container or can be frozen for up to 6 months.

MAKES 40

walnut fingers

MOROCCANS ARE RATHER DEVOTED TO SWEETMEATS WRAPPED IN TISSUE PAPER-LIKE PASTRY. THIS IS A CLASSIC COMPOSITION — THE FILLING CAN CONTAIN EITHER A GROUND ALMOND OR WALNUT PASTE OR SOMETIMES A DATE OR FIG PASTE.

1 cup walnut pieces
2 tablespoons caster sugar
1 teaspoon ground cinnamon
2 tablespoons liquid honey
1 teaspoon orange flower water
4 sheets filo pastry
50g butter, melted

1　Preheat oven to 190°C. Place walnuts in a food processor and pulse to chop. Add sugar, cinnamon, honey and orange flower water and process to form a solid ball of mixture. Divide the nut mixture into 12 and roll each portion into a 9cm-long sausage shape.

2　Lay a sheet of filo pastry on a work surface and brush lightly with melted butter. Place another sheet on top and cut this into 6 even-sized squares. Repeat with the remaining 2 sheets of filo, so you end up with 12 squares.

3　Butter the edges of a square of filo, place one nut shape at one end. Fold in 1cm along both sides of pastry to secure filling and roll up like a cigar. Brush outer surface lightly with butter and place on a baking tray. Repeat with remaining squares of filo.

4　Bake for 15 minutes or until golden brown. Remove to a wire rack to cool.

MAKES 12

WALNUT FINGERS

PRUNE AND ALMOND ICE-CREAM

prune and almond ice-cream

THIS ICE-CREAM IS NOT TRADITIONAL; IT IS MY OWN INTERPRETATION THAT EMBRACES A FEW OF THE
VITAL FLAVOURS OF MOROCCO.

2 eggs
1/4 cup sugar
300ml cream
1/2 cup ground almonds
1 teaspoon ground cinnamon
1 cup chopped pitted prunes

1   Place eggs and sugar in a bowl set over a saucepan of gently
    simmering water and whisk with an electric beater until mixture
    is very thick and pale (this takes at least 5 minutes). Remove
    from the heat and continue whisking for at least 5 minutes
    more until the mixture has cooled.

2   Whip the cream until soft peaks hold their shape. Gently fold
    almonds, cinnamon and prunes into the cream, then fold in
    egg mixture. Pour into a 1-litre lidded container, cover tightly
    and freeze overnight until firm.

3   Scoop ice-cream into balls to serve.

SERVES 8

dates stuffed with rose and almond paste

IT IS INTERESTING TO NOTE THAT PASTRIES AND SWEETMEATS SUCH AS THESE ARE NOT SERVED AT THE
END OF A MEAL IN MOROCCO BUT ARE GENERALLY RESERVED FOR SPECIAL OCCASIONS OR VISITORS.

12 fresh dates
1/2 cup blanched whole almonds
1/4 cup caster sugar
1–2 drops pink food colouring
1 teaspoon rose water

1   Slit the surface of each date lengthways to remove and
    discard the stones.

2   Place the almonds in a food processor and grind finely. Add
    sugar, food colouring and rose water and process to combine
    to a ball of paste, adding a teaspoonful of cold water if the
    mixture is too dry. Divide this mixture into 12 portions.

3   Shape each portion of almond paste into an almond shape
    and wedge this into the date to fill the space where the stone
    once sat. Some of the almond paste should show between
    the slit sides of the date. Cut a lattice pattern into the almond
    paste to decorate, if desired.

MAKES 12

roses

Moroccans are partial to sumptuously scented foods and will use, among other spices, dried rose petals and diminutive rose-buds to flavour sweet and savoury dishes alike. Rose petals are included in some pastries or made into a sugar syrup to drench others, and rose petal jam is eaten as a spoon-sweet. The ground petals are contained in the complex spice mix, ras el hanout (see page 57), used to flavour tagines and game dishes. Handfuls of tiny dried rose-buds can be used for making a sweet-scented tea infusion. To deliciously perfume the house, the perfumed buds can be scattered in small dishes (like pot-pourri) and placed in rooms to release their haunting fragrance. These pretty little rose-buds can be easily purchased from spice souks, where they are sold loose from huge sacks.

The delightful 'rose of Damascus' was brought from Persia by the Arabs and is the variety that is now cultivated in profusion in the Dadès, Todra and Ferkla valleys of Morocco. These fertile valleys are filled with masses of rose bushes that yield thousands of tons of full, fragrant pink petals each year. The concentrated aromatic essential oil of rose is extracted from the harvested petals, and rose water is produced by distillation. Rose water is an important flavouring ingredient in many different Moroccan sweets and pastries. It is also used as a perfumed toilet water.

After a Moroccan meal, guests may be offered rose water to cleanse their hands. Being sprinkled with this voluptuously scented water, dispensed from the nozzle of an ornately decorated, slender silver bottle, is a truly sensuous thrill. The tingling coolness of water on hot skin, combined with the elation of breathing floral air and the satisfaction of participating in an age-old ritual are heady sensations that linger long after leaving Morocco. To experience this ceremony for the first time is like being presented with a rare and unexpected gift. JLEC

travel notes

TRAVELLING IN MOROCCO may take some adjusting to but essentially this fascinating land rewards independent travellers well.

time to travel

We chose to tour Morocco in the off-season. January in Morocco is generally warmer during the day and cooler at night; there are substantially fewer tourists; off-season hotel rates apply, and few if any sights/highlights are closed to the public.

hotels

With patience and a smile, substantial discounts can be achieved from the hotel rack rates. Often the best way in more remote areas is to choose the hotel's half-board rate (bed and breakfast). In the cities there are usually smart, clean and incredibly cheap cafés near most hotels, which offer fresh and tasty food and are worth a visit for the experience alone.

booking a riad (traditional house within the medina)

Fez is only now adopting Marrakech's time-proven concept of renting riads. Consequently a number of the newer entrants into the riad-renting business have much to learn about western creature comforts. It is advisable to confirm that you require such essentials as heating (important in winter when the temperature plummets to below zero and the central courtyard is open to

the heavens), beds as opposed to wool-filled bench seating, sheets, pillows (non-wool filled), blankets, soap (unwrapped and unused), hot water, water pressure, and whether the owners will be spending the night in the house.

eating out

Moroccans generally prefer to eat at home so restaurants often offer tourist menus. The best advice is to befriend a trusty local and be invited to their home for an evening meal.

wine

We recommend Celliers de Meknes wines, which taste better than they sound. They have the added benefit of being as soft on the pocket as they are on the palate in this dry Muslim state where the consumption of alcohol is not encouraged. Our favourites were the merlot cabernet sauvignon, and the rosé to accompany chicken couscous.

bartering

Bartering is expected in Morocco and can be done in a friendly yet spirited manner, and expect the final price to be some-where between 25–50 per cent less than first asked. It pays to shop around and compare prices – a bit of knowledge will give you an edge when negotiating. Be gracious and polite.

items to look for

Earthenware tagines and other pottery items, ceramic tiles, embroidered linen, textiles, home furnishings, lamps, leather-wear and slippers, antiques, wood products and wrought-iron.

the souks

Don't accept free 'presents' from henna tattooists, silver-bangle purveyors or any others of a similar ilk. It is easy to fall for the oldest selling trick on the street: your 'present' may well become the subject of a heated discussion with a big burly chap at the end of the lane who will accuse you of stealing the goods. Worse still is the perseverance of the henna women, whose only thought in life once the 'present' has been applied is to hound you mercilessly for a 'gift' (money) in return. They may wear you down in the end, and with their amazing memories it will then not be safe to go into the medina ever again without being hounded. The morning is the best time to visit the souks of Marrakech, before they become too crowded and busy. Late in the day, between 7–8 p.m. is also a quiet time. A bonus is that stall-holders are often more open to firmer bargaining at the end of the day. Touts and unauthorised guides have been officially outlawed. However, now the tour groups have a well-defined path past (and into) the shops that are of benefit to their guides' pocket. So if you want to see the real medina, take any one of the hundreds of paths to anywhere other than where they are heading. If you get lost, and you will, there is always a child who will be willing to lead you out of the maze for a small reward.

crossing a road

We were advised to walk really slowly onto the road and wait for the cars to drive around us – this is nerve-racking at first but it works. Never use a pedestrian crossing as this seems to be an indication to Moroccan drivers to drive even more erratically.

taxis

Fleets of colourful petit taxis (little taxis) make transport easy in most Moroccan cities. Very few petit taxis have meters, so it's necessary to either barter beforehand or on arrival, but you'll find most drivers will happily accept the going rate. Ask at the Tourist Information Office or your hotel concierge for standard fares. Where there are horse-drawn carriage taxis (Marrakech, for instance), the fares are generally about the same price as for petit taxis, although it is still advisable to agree on a price beforehand.

photographs

All women, and many men and children, object to their photograph being taken because they think that either part of their spirit will be taken away, or that once the photographs are in another land people will laugh at their image. However, using discretion, a genuine smile and a request of 'OK saw-a?' (OK photo?) more often than not you will be rewarded with the photograph opportunity that you desire. Do not take photographs of beggars or the impoverished side of life under any circumstances. Quite rightfully, the inhabitants want an appropriate view of Morocco shown to the world. Always ask if you want more than a general shot in public. If money or a gift is asked for, then establish the amount prior to taking the photograph, otherwise lengthy and embarrassing negotiations and protestations may ensue afterwards.

---

glossary

amelou a mixture of ground almonds bound with argan oil and honey, and eaten on bread for breakfast or as a snack

argan tree native to North Africa; the seeds of the fruit of the argan tree are pressed for their oil

aubergine French name for eggplant

beghrir specialty bread

b'stilla traditional dish of Morocco; basically a sweet-savoury pie of pigeon wrapped in a special type of paper-thin pastry called wharka

bab monumental gate

babouches slippers

Berber indigenous inhabitants of Morocco

brochette adopted French name for skewered meats or kebabs

caïdal traditional tent

couscousière a special-shaped double boiler for cooking couscous

djellabah traditional pointy-hooded, ankle-length garment worn principally by men

fava broad beans

haik a single piece of cloth worn by women in public as an all-encompassing wrap

hammam traditional steam room

harissa fiery chilli and spice paste, originally from Tunisia

harsha specialty bread

ka'b ghzal famous Moroccan pastry shaped like the slender ankle of a gazelle

kahwa nuss u nuss coffee with milk; proportioned literally 'half and half'

kasar fortified rural village, tightly crammed within protective walls

kasbah fortified rural dwelling made of mud-bricks

kefta meatballs or flavoured mincemeat moulded onto skewers

khodinja spiced tea

khubz bread

m'choui authentic Berber lamb dish where a whole seasoned lamb is roasted on a spit in a mud-oven pit

maghreb literally translates to 'where the sun sets'; term used to encompass the lands of Morocco, Algeria and Tunisia

Marabout the title given to a religious leader or saint and their tombs

mastic aromatic tree gum, powdered and used as a spice in sweet dishes and breads

medina old town or city completely enclosed within defensive walls (ramparts)

Mellah Jewish area or quarter within the medina

mezze a way of eating; a series of small dishes or pleasant tastes – there are as many different mezze dishes as there are cooks to invent them

mlaoui specialty bread

msammen specialty bread

muezzin Muslim caller to prayers

palmerie oasis filled with palm trees

pisé both a rocky flat desert and the earth and stone mixture used as a building material

riad an inside garden or courtyard; this term is now also applied to traditional guest-houses within the medina

sellou sweetmeat

shisha a hubbly-bubbly water pipe

souk any market or collection of stalls whether transient or permanent; in some towns, souks take place on a specific day of the week, others are permanently established within the medina

tagine refers both to the ceramic-cooking vessel with a conical lid and the finished dish, which is essentially a stew

thé à la menthe mint tea, the national drink of Morocco

tizi mountain pass

ville nouvelle a new city set up apart from the ancient medina

wadi river course – be it dry or flowing

wharka specialised pastry leaves used for making b'stilla and other traditional pastry dishes

spain

mediterranean sea

N

atlantic ocean

tangier

RIF

rabat

meknes

CASABLANCA

FEZ

EL JADIDA

AZEMMOUR

MIDDLE ATLAS

safi

MIDELT

er-rachidia

ESSAOUIRA

aït-benhaddou

TODRA GORGE

MARRAKECH

HIGH ATLAS

ERFOUD

tinerhir

rissani

skoura

OUARZAZATE

TAROUDANNT

ANTI ATLAS

algeria

morocco

index

Our heartfelt thanks go to the following people for their help and assistance:

Rachid Lamrani, our Moroccan tour guide, font of knowledge and effortless adapter to the needs of his clients. Thanks also go to Rachid's mother, Fatima el Hatimi and Fatima el Azhari, a friend of the Lamrani family, for giving up an entire day with a smile and inspired skill, along with their age-old cooking secrets. And grateful thanks to all the talented Moroccan cooks we met, for sharing their time and recipes with us.

We are grateful to Kasbah Agafay and Small Luxury Hotels of the World for providing us with an opportunity to experience staying in an oasis of calm, luxury and the very best of all that is Morocco – both present and past. And to chef Ahmed Howard Doulaki for demonstrating his authentic recipes.

And thank you to the people of Morocco, for letting us into your lives, secrets, land and history.

Thank you James Irving for providing 24-hour on-call travel agency service that was, once again, way beyond the norm.

We wish to thank Gulf Air, in particular Crammer Ball, General Manager Australia, for ensuring that we were able to experience the joy of travelling with ultimate ease, service and comfort.

Our warmest thanks go to the wonderful people at Penguin Books (NZ) for making sure that this book happened in the first place. Bernice Beachman and Philippa Gerrard – once again you made the seemingly impossible possible. And thank you Athena Sommerfeld, award-winning designer, for distilling a mountain of material into a work of art.

Thank you Anna Bougen for ensuring that the areas of security and translation were managed to perfection, for assisting with prop collection and for your great companionship and sense of humour.

And to our other travel companions – Peter Fulton, Graeme Edwards, Stuart and Gilly Huggett – thanks for your company, hospitality and for understanding the vagaries of book research and photography.

Contact details.

Rachid Lamrani (official Moroccan tour guide)
Rachid_lamrani@hotmail.com

Kasbah Agafay www.kasbahagafay.com
Route de L'airport BP 226
40000 Marrakech Medina
Morocco
Kasbah Agafay is a member of 'Small Luxury Hotels of the World'
www.slh.com

Gulf Air www.gulfairco.com

James Irving jirving@mtatravel.com.au

PENGUIN BOOKS
Published by the Penguin Group
Penguin Group (NZ), cnr Airborne and Rosedale
Roads, Albany, Auckland 1310, New Zealand
(a division of Pearson New Zealand Ltd)
Penguin Group (USA) Inc., 375 Hudson Street,
New York, New York 10014, USA
Penguin Group (Canada), 10 Alcorn Avenue, Toronto,
Ontario, Canada M4V 3B2 (a division of Pearson
Penguin Canada Inc.)
Penguin Books Ltd, 80 Strand, London,
WC2R 0RL, England
Penguin Ireland, 25 St Stephen's Green,
Dublin 2, Ireland (a division of Penguin Books Ltd)
Penguin Group (Australia), 250 Camberwell Road,
Camberwell, Victoria 3124, Australia (a division of
Pearson Australia Group Pty Ltd)
Penguin Books India Pvt Ltd, 11, Community Centre,
Panchsheel Park, New Delhi - 110 017, India
Penguin Books (South Africa) (Pty) Ltd, 24 Sturdee
Avenue, Rosebank, Johannesburg 2196, South Africa

Penguin Books Ltd, Registered Offices: 80 Strand,
London, WC2R 0RL, England

First published by Penguin Group (NZ), 2004
3 5 7 9 10 8 6 4 2

Designed and typeset by Athena Sommerfeld
Prepress by microdot
Printed in China through Bookbuilders, Hong Kong

ISBN 0 14 301942 2
A catalogue record for this book is available from the
National Library of New Zealand.

www.penguin.co.nz